M000226576

Learning How to Hope

Learning How to Hope

Reviving Democracy through Our Schools and Civil Society

SARAH M. STITZLEIN

OXFORD

UNIVERSITY PRESS

OXFORD
UNIVERSITY PRESS

Oxford University Press is a department of the University of Oxford. It furthers
the University's objective of excellence in research, scholarship, and education
by publishing worldwide. Oxford is a registered trade mark of Oxford University
Press in the UK and certain other countries.

Published in the United States of America by Oxford University Press
198 Madison Avenue, New York, NY 10016, United States of America.

CIP data is on file at the Library of Congress
ISBN 978–0–19–006265–1

1 3 5 7 9 8 6 4 2

Printed by Sheridan Books, Inc., United States of America

Contents

Acknowledgments

A few years ago, shortly after my only child was born and I had just moved across the country, leaving behind a place and job I loved, I experienced a terrible event in my personal life. I went to see a therapist. He asked me to explain what had happened. As I laid out the details and described the difficulties I was experiencing as a result, I also spoke of the future and what I could do to make things better. When I stopped, the therapist said, "In my 25 years in this line of work, I've never met someone more hopeful than you are." I was a bit taken aback by this comment, unsure of whether it was actually a jab at me for being naïve in the face of an awful situation or whether it was a compliment about the outlook I maintained even in that predicament. I responded with a line that I shared with many concerned friends at the time, "I cannot change that this happened to me, but I can determine how I respond to it." I left, wondering, "what makes me so hopeful and how might I nurture hope in others?" I realized that my hopefulness extended well beyond my personal life and into my civic and political life also. This book is the result of those reflections, questions that were magnified as I looked at the hopelessness many people have experienced recently within American democracy. Certainly, there have been many friends and family along the way, more than I can name here, who have supported my hopeful demeanor. This includes my mother, who passed suddenly during the final stages of completing this book and whose death has once again brought me back to the more difficult moments of sustaining personal hope and yet also helped me see her as an important influence on my inclination to hope. And there have been teachers who have identified and cultivated my habits of hope. I'm grateful to each of you. May you continue to do so for others.

I thank my graduate assistants, Melissa Knueven, Carrie Nolan, and, especially, Lori Foote, for their assistance in preparing this book. I also thank Lisa Sibbett and Karen Zaino for reading the manuscript and providing the insights of a social studies teacher and English teacher. I have benefited from helpful feedback from fellow philosophers of education Kathy Hytten, Winston Thompson, and Carrie Nolan. I also appreciated the discussions of my work when I spoke about political hope in the Life of the Mind lecture at the University of Cincinnati; the Boyd Bode Memorial Lecture at the Ohio State University; the Templeton Foundation's Glass Half Full Collaboratory in Estes Park, Colorado; and the New Directions in the Philosophy of Hope Conference at Goethe University in Germany. I am grateful for financial support from the Templeton Foundation, Society for the Advancement of American Philosophy, and the Center for Ethics & Education. Support for an open access publishing grant came from the Toward an Open Monograph Ecosystem, funded by the Association of American Universities, the Association of Research Libraries, and the Association of American University Presses. Finally, thanks to the following journals, who granted permission to print significantly revised and expanded versions of earlier articles.

Stitzlein, Sarah M. "Hoping and Democracy," *Contemporary Pragmatism*, 15, no. 2 (2018): 1–24.

Stitzlein, Sarah M. "Teaching for Hope in the Era of Grit," *Teachers College Record*, 120, no. 3 (2018).

Foote, Lori, and Sarah M. Stitzlein. "Teaching Hope: Cultivating Pragmatist Habits," *The Journal of School & Society*, 3, no. 2 (2016): 32–40.

Nolan, Carrie, and Sarah M. Stitzlein. "Meaningful Hope for Teachers in Times of High Anxiety and Low Morale," *Democracy & Education*, 19, no. 1 (2011): 1–10.

Learning How to Hope

1

Hope in America?

The very idea of democracy, the meaning of democracy, must be continually explored afresh; it has to be constantly discovered and rediscovered, remade and reorganized; while the political and economic and social institutions in which it is embodied have to be remade and reorganized to meet the changes that are going on in the development of new needs on the part of human beings and new resources for satisfying these needs.

—John Dewey[1]

Hope is at the heart of democracy. Hope animates life in a democracy, moving citizens forward through new challenges, new ideas, and new experiments. When we are hopeless, and especially when we are in despair, not only are our individual lives more difficult but also our social and political lives suffer. We find ourselves disempowered, unable to solve shared problems and create improved ways of living and working together. The American presidential elections of 2008 and 2016 marked significant shifts in how our polarized citizenry experiences both hope and despair. Some citizens excitedly anticipated considerable improvement in their lives as a result of their preferred candidate's victory, while some backers of losing candidates feared the worst. As each presidential term played out, many citizens on both sides of the aisle found themselves increasingly disappointed with the leader representing their political party, and their positive outlook for the well-being of the country waned.

As presidential eras move on and new election seasons arrive, we are left asking, "Are there reasons to hope?," "How can I hope?," and "What should I hope for?" The answers are often shaped by our political environment and educational experiences. In this book, I will examine how addressing these questions in today's social and political context suggests not only reasons for *why* we can hope and particular content of *what* we ought to hope for but

Learning How to Hope. Sarah M. Stitzlein, Oxford University Press (2020). © Oxford University Press.
DOI: 10.1093/oso/9780190062651.001.0001

also, more importantly, an enriched understanding of *how* we hope together. I will argue that such shared work is more fruitful than mere independent wishes, optimism, or—increasingly popular in education circles—grit. I'm speaking here of substantial hopes for our future together as citizens and for our lives in America today, such as hoping for equal treatment of all citizens under the law or an economy that provides opportunities and economic mobility for everyone. These differ from insignificant hopes, which are often fleeting or relatively inconsequential, like hoping I'll get to shake hands with my favorite candidate on a campaign stop in my town.

Hope is seemingly well known and widely experienced, yet its source, cultivation, and relationship to democracy are all worthy of more careful investigation. This is especially the case in politically contentious times, when citizens tend to hitch their hope on particular politicians and find themselves increasingly divided from those endorsing the other party's leaders. America has historically tended to think of itself as a beacon of hope. Indeed, many countries and immigrants have long looked to us in that spirit and many of our political leaders have aimed to inspire us by referencing that image in their speeches. We celebrate America as a place where people set out to forge a new and better way of life, buoyed by promises of liberty, equality, and opportunity for all—though too many of us ignore that those ideals have not been fairly extended to everyone. But, an array of anecdotes and data suggest that many Americans, including the youngest generations, are now struggling to hope. Examples ranging from rampant opioid addiction to rising suicide rates suggest that aspects of hope and despair stretch far beyond our elections or our frustrations with political leaders and deep into our personal lives.[2] If hope is waning in America, our very identity as a country, our sense of ourselves within it, and our role in the world may be at risk. Moreover, our well-being as individuals and as a citizenry may be in danger.

This book does not make a call to return to American roots, as though there was a time when the American Ideal was pure and the American Dream was possible for all. It does, however, highlight some of the best of what our past has to offer as a source for moving forward. It is a present- and future-directed endeavor that grapples with past and current struggles. Those include recognition that the American Ideals, represented in our key principles of democracy, have long been tied up with white supremacy, economic disparity, and other problematic power relations that have made life and hope in America much more difficult for some citizens than others. My intent in this book is to help resuscitate hope within America by offering a notion of hope that is grounded in real struggles. It is an account that grows out of philosophical pragmatism, a tradition deeply tied to both our country's history and democratic ways of life. Despite the religious history of our nation, it is not a hope that transcends this world through appeals to God. But, believing in God may help some Americans pursue a better future by buttressing their resolve, providing visions of how we might live more justly, and uniting them with fellow believers in communities not only of worship but also of civic involvement. Instead, it is a hope that is related to *our* experiences and *our* agency (our ability to participate in and impact democratic life). It is a hope that can be cultivated among our citizenry.

As we move into the 2020 election, I aim to focus less on political leaders and more on our own actions to improve our lives and country. Along the way, I intend to offer insight into how we might identify leaders who may better support our efforts as citizens, so that hoping becomes something that we do together, and that is sustainable from one election to the next— regardless of the winning party or candidate. Importantly, I aim to shift our focus to future generations and how we might cultivate hope within them so that they take an active role in leading America through times of despair and struggle by using hope as a unifying force. For that reason, I will turn later in this book to looking at citizenship education in particular, a key venue for teaching hope and learning habits of democratic living. *I argue that schools and civil society should nurture hope as a set of habits that disposes citizens toward possibility and motivates citizens to act to improve their lives and, often, those of others.*[3] These habits are flexible, adapting to our changing world so that long after our current struggles in American democracy have faded and new ones have developed, habits of hope will likely have lasting relevance and usefulness. As such, this project of teaching hope, while grounded in present struggles, is aimed at sustaining and improving democracy well into the future.

More than a Campaign Slogan

Democracy, as Walt Whitman said, is "a great word whose history remains unwritten."[4] Hope helps us write the story of democracy because it shapes the future we envision and pursue. As we chart that course, America unfolds as a venture that often requires bold vision, action, and collaboration. Early in our history, we recognized the precarious nature of our experiment, and we worked hard to bolster it by proclaiming the benefits of democracy through political speeches, documents, and monuments. We foregrounded the development of good citizens within our schools based on our hope of preserving and expanding democracy among our ranks.[5] This was most pronounced in the bills justifying the expansion of public schooling written by Thomas Jefferson, who hoped to bring education to a wider demographic and to better prepare citizens for the responsibilities of self-government. These aims were furthered during the common school movement of the 1800s propelled by Horace Mann, who sought to develop a shared American identity in growing citizens by enrolling an even larger population. While those celebrations of and missions to improve democracy have dissipated in recent decades, hope has lingered as we craft the story of democracy. Most notably, we see hope used as a campaign slogan and within our political rhetoric—perhaps a sign of its appeal to citizens and of its need within democracy.

Hope took center stage in Barack Obama's 2008 presidential campaign, as supporters donned now iconic t-shirts adorned with Obama's face and the simple word: "HOPE." But on the campaign trail, hope traces a longer history. I offer here only a brief glimpse of candidates in recent decades who have emphasized hope during their campaigns, and I reveal some of the ways in which they have employed hope. Let's begin with John F. Kennedy, whose zest and youthful looks complemented his message of hope borne out through public action. Riding to victory on a Frank Sinatra campaign tune titled "High Hopes," JFK directed our attention not toward the glory of America's past but rather to a vision of what America "someday can, and through the efforts of us all, someday will be."[6] And to achieve that future, his inaugural address famously implored, "Ask not what your country will do for you—ask what you can do for your country."

During Bill Clinton's nomination speech, he recalled listening to JFK's "summons to citizenship" as a teenager. Trying to breathe fresh life into that sentiment, he spoke of the work ahead as citizens aimed to improve life in America, chanting five times: "We can do it."[7] That proclamation was later revived by Obama, who routinely exhorted crowds to join him in a chorus of "Yes, we can!" Like Clinton before him, Obama found hope for the future by looking at what Americans had achieved in the past, bolstering his confidence that America can continue to be improved. As he accepted the presidential nomination, Obama claimed, "Our union can be perfected. What we've already achieved gives us hope for what we can and must achieve tomorrow."[8]

While many candidates offered a vague and indeterminate sense of hope through their speeches and slogans, Obama attempted to articulate some of the common hopes of Americans. A tour of America led him to conclude: "at the core of the American experience are a set of ideals that continue to stir our collective conscience; a common set of values that bind us together despite our differences; a running thread of hope that makes our improbable experiment in democracy work."[9] During his victory speech, he laid out what some of those specific hopes are, including things, such as good schools for our children, and particular ways of life, such as showing compassion for others. He argued that identifying our common hopes is a useful way to move America forward through political divisiveness, racism, and other struggles.[10] Like JFK, Obama insisted that hope requires courageous action on behalf of citizens.

> I've never been more hopeful about our future. I have never been more hopeful about America. And I ask you to sustain that hope. I'm not talking about blind optimism—the kind of hope that just ignores the enormity of the tasks ahead or the roadblocks that stand in our path. I'm not talking about the wishful idealism that allows us to just sit on the sidelines or shirk from a fight. I have always believed that hope is that stubborn thing inside us that insists, despite all the evidence to the contrary, that something better awaits us, so long as we have the courage to keep reaching, to keep working, to keep fighting.[11]

While the idea of hope was more pronounced within the campaigns of Democrats in recent decades, it has also played a role in those of Republicans. They invoked moving imagery to symbolize hope while also showing, like their Democratic counterparts, that hope required effort to support and improve America. Ronald Reagan spoke often of America as the shining "city on the hill" that was a symbol of hope and freedom for immigrants and countries around the world. He chose to conclude his farewell speech with that image and reflections on how Americans had made our country a better place during his presidency.[12] George H. W. Bush later followed, describing citizens and volunteer organizations hard at work to improve America as "a thousand points of light."[13] Then, his son George W. Bush ran on the slogan, "A safer world and a more hopeful America."

Tapping in to the idea that hope requires an initial sense of security before one can explore and build a better America, some Republican candidates, including John McCain and Donald Trump, focused on protection. In 2016, Trump sought to assure economic security as well as the physical safety of Americans from the threats he perceived from terrorists and some immigrants. In light of increased poverty and a standard of living that had remained relatively flat for the last three decades, many economically struggling Americans found hope in Trump. While Trump's campaign may have been setting a stage for hope, many of his speeches sought to engage and rally voters by focusing on the severity of our country's problems.[14] Unlike his Democratic and Republican forerunners who drew on both the promises and the shortcomings of the past as justification for inventing a better future together, Trump claimed he would bring about a better life on behalf of Americans. He positioned himself as a strongman who both knew what was best for Americans and who would do the will of the people.

A reporter interviewed visitors to Washington, DC, during the weekend of the inauguration and Women's March in 2017, asking what each citizen was hopeful for and what they were going to do as a result of that hope.[15] Citizens on the right shared stories of excitement about reclaiming an American past that they believed to be better than the present, especially in terms of economics and military power. They expressed confidence that President Trump would make things better and vowed to back him. On the left, some citizens were emotionally reeling in the aftermath of the surprising election outcome. They worried that Trump might bring harm to particular identity groups that he disparaged during the election, including women and immigrants. They called for interest groups to come together in resistance and urged others to volunteer on behalf of people at risk, to donate to groups championing those identity groups, and to become active in politics, especially at the local level. In the center were people who were troubled by the divides in American politics and who chose to engage in civic action and dialogue in hopes of working across differences. Each interviewee across the political spectrum was trying to articulate a reason and a way to hope, and many had defined content of what they hoped for already in mind. Perhaps some interviewees sensed that hope is too often a political slogan used in passive recitation, but that doesn't require one to actually *do* more than cast a vote and perhaps donate to a campaign. Perhaps some recognized, as I argue in these pages, that democracy requires a deeper and more sustainable form of hope that is enacted and endures long after the polls close and inaugural balls end.

Changes in Democracy and Our Citizenry

Before looking at what hope means and how we can cultivate it, let's first briefly take stock of current conditions that relate to hopelessness in political life. While recognizing the interplay between personal hopelessness and political outlook, I will focus on hopelessness as it relates to democracy, as my primary aim is to revive democracy as a whole, though of course this depends on bolstering the hope of individual citizens also. This is especially the case when democracy is understood in a participatory sense, relying on the contributions, efforts, and deliberations of the individuals who compose it.

Given my focus on political life, I speak of citizens. But in an era when defining a citizen is increasingly contentious and avenues for becoming a citizen are increasingly limited, I want to be sure that I am not misunderstood. I am not drawing the boundaries of citizenship as a legal status of where one lives, is born, or what rights and services one is entitled to. Rather, I talk more broadly about citizenship as a social and political identity and practices that may not reflect one's legal or documented status. I want to be inclusive here because I recognize that hope is relevant for everyone and may be especially important for those who are struggling to even be recognized or valued in America. The task of restoring hope and reviving democracy requires an all-hands-on-deck approach, and I know that even those who may not qualify as legal citizens can significantly shape and improve American social and political life.

In pragmatist spirit, the account I offer in this book must attend to real conditions—recognizing their constraints, complexities, and possibilities. Unfortunately, these are conditions where hope is struggling, where elements of democracy may be in jeopardy, and where the hope that is present is largely privatized—confined to just our personal pursuits, often for economic or material well-being. While I do not want to overstate current problems in the way that citizens as a whole view democracy and its stability, I highlight here some of the more worrisome patterns emerging among certain populations in order to uncover problematic potential trends and to head them off with the ideas I put forward in this book.

To begin, two prominent interpreters of a recent study using the World Values Survey and other polling sources found that democratic citizens have "become more cynical about the value of democracy as a political system, less hopeful that anything they do might influence public policy, and more willing to express support for authoritarian alternatives."[16] Those citizens have increasingly withdrawn from participating in formal processes of democracy, such as citizen ballot initiatives or even voting, and from activities in the public or civil spheres, such as joining in organizations or protests.[17] There has been a dramatic shift in how the wealthy view democracy, in particular, with 16% of them now believing that military rule is a better way of living and an astounding 35% of rich young Americans holding such a view.[18]

Globally, after widespread growth of both liberal and electoral democracies and their values in the last quarter of the twentieth century and into the beginning of the twenty-first, the tide has turned. "The year 2016 was the eleventh straight year in which countries suffering net declines in political and civil liberties outnumbered the gainers. In nearly all these years, the losses substantially exceeded the gains."[19] Support for democracy has receded and support for authoritarianism has increased. Yet, roughly a quarter of people across thirty-eight major countries polled in 2017, including the United States, remain committed to democracy.[20] Within those countries, those with the highest levels of education are more likely to endorse a representative democracy, while those with the least education are more likely to support a military government, including 24% of Americans with a secondary education or less.[21] Additionally, those who see the past as better than the present are less satisfied with how democracy is working.[22] When looking at American Millennials born between 1980 and the mid-1990s in particular, 35% say they are losing faith in democracy, with percentages even higher for black and Hispanic Millennials.[23]

Critics of some interpretations of the World Values Survey and other polling data point out that these trends may reflect mere lifecycle issues that we've seen before, where younger people tend to show stronger signs of disaffection across decades, rather than a trend toward decreasing support for democracy as a whole.[24] Indeed, many of the strongest supporters of populist-authoritarian parties are actually older, and often, poorer, citizens.[25] Many of them increasingly feel "left behind," with unmet needs and concerns unrecognized by mainstream political leaders.[26] Some social commentators argue that a significant portion of the American population increasingly feels economically trapped and jealous of others (often perceived to be immigrant or minorities) who seem to be getting some advantages that are moving them ahead, such as lax immigration laws or affirmative action. As a result, they feel fear, resentment, and distrust toward others, focus on looking out for themselves, group with those who feel similarly slighted, and seek leaders who will reassert their position of power within society.[27] While some people may dismiss mere feelings, the experiences of perceiving oneself as left behind has real consequences, including harmful actions, in our country. Regardless of the debate around how the World Values Survey should be interpreted and the level of alarm it raises, there are clearly issues of concern when it comes to the hopelessness of some of our citizens and the outlook for democracy.

Leaders Fall Short and Citizens Become Passive

There are likely many factors impacting this current state of affairs, and I will touch on just a few here. First, some recent American presidential candidates ran on messages of hope and yet the visions evoked have often failed to be fulfilled in reality, crushing the heightened expectations of citizens.[28] Federal and local politicians often use the rhetoric of hope, but they tend to distort what hope really is and what it requires of citizens. Instead, they may make reference to the supposed destiny of the nation with God as its backer. Sometimes those politicians put forward goals that aren't sufficiently based in evidence or reality to be feasibly achieved, don't arise from the citizens themselves, are not well understood by the citizens, or are not held open to revision or criticism.[29] Or, as in the cases of Barack Obama and Donald Trump, some citizens place their hope in the leader himself, invoking a messianic figure who will save the country. The promises of democracy are also coming up short. While some people see liberal democracy as a good in itself, most celebrate it for the freedom and prosperity it typically brings.[30] When those promises are unfulfilled, some citizens begin to doubt not only the leaders but also the system.[31]

I will argue that, rather than passively relying on the hope promised by politicians and being disappointed by shortcomings, citizens must participate in shaping and fulfilling hope. Rather than hitching hope and overall support for democracy to a leader's fulfillment of campaign promises, this approach makes hope more genuine and robust. It changes the nature of the game, from spectator sport, where armchair quarterbacks bemoan the failed attempts of others, to active participation in a team working toward goals together.

Hope for Some, But Not for Others

A second factor influencing the current state of hope and democracy is structural violence and inequality, which is exacerbated by interpersonal and community-based violence. Common among poor and racial minority communities in America, such injustice has wreaked havoc on hope.[32] In some cases, it has rendered hope exhausting.[33] Many marginalized citizens are told that they must never give up hope and that they must keep trying to earn a better life for themselves, in part through improving their own character regardless of the stagnant harmful practices of others. As a result, many of those citizens are left either hopeless or perpetually chasing a vision of justice that is out of reach, while some turn inward to their racial, ethnic, or other local communities to engage in alternative practices that bring hope and forms of civil engagement that may not always be recognized by dominant groups.[34] Poor citizens, in particular, sometimes get so entrenched in attending to every little economic crisis along the way (How will I pay to fix my flat tire so I can get to work tomorrow? How will I afford back-to-school supplies?) that they have neither the time, energy, or resources to plan for a better long-term future or for the future of our country as a whole, thereby making it hard to engage in hope or in democracy.

These struggles take a toll on both physical and mental health. Indeed, medical science has revealed that prolonged experiences of pain and hardship amplify hopelessness by causing the body to release neurochemicals that disable us from feeling positive.[35] Within children in particular, structural violence has been shown to cause rage, aggression, depression, and fatalism. Those mental and physical struggles spill over into the classroom, negatively impacting academic achievement and civic engagement.[36] And children of color commit suicide at higher rates than their white peers. Yet, black and Hispanic adults are likely to retain a generally more optimistic outlook than their poor white counterparts, many of whom lack cultural supports, see few opportunities for economic advancement, and seek avenues for escape, leading to what some have dubbed "despair deaths" through suicide and overdose.[37]

While white despair deaths have become increasingly visible and acknowledged across the country, especially in the midst of a rash of opioid addiction, the struggles of black and Latino people are largely unacknowledged by mainstream America. Sometimes this is because dominant people are unaware of the struggles of those living in what African American Studies scholar Eddie Glaude calls "opportunity deserts." But many times, those more powerful people insidiously ignore what is happening in those black communities, in particular, a reflection of a long history of placing less value on the lives and well-being of black citizens. Those communities, Glaude explains, are

> places of tremendous hardship, joblessness, and what seems to be perma-
> nent marginalization. Opportunity deserts are those communities, both
> urban and rural, that lack the resources and public institutions that give
> those who live there a chance to reach beyond their current lives. They are
> characterized, in part, by (1) the absence of social networks that point out
> pathways for professional and educational advance and (2) heightened po-
> lice surveillance that increases the likelihood of someone's landing in the
> criminal justice system.[38]

Within these communities, black citizens struggle to hope under such limiting conditions that constrain one's ability to imagine and pursue better lives. Though Glaude speaks only of black communities, these opportunity deserts likely extend into other nondominant racial and ethnic communities. Moreover, white people who perpetuate living in ignorance or denial of black and other minority suffering, fail to see the hope-shattering patterns of their own behavior which reflect valuing some lives more than others, thereby further inhibiting sustainable hope in those struggling communities. And when those same people insist that black folks and other minority people should keep on hoping and do not recognize that democratic ideas of liberty, equality, and opportunity have long been unjustly distributed in America, they propagate conditions of harm and exhaustion. Inequality of hope, dem-ocratic participation, and well-being in America will continue to be rigged as long as we continue to deny the many ways in which our country has valued some people over others.[39]

Disconnection and Distrust

Third, citizenship in America has increasingly become focused on personal responsibility, entrepreneurship, and private success. Historical accounts of rugged individualism have now joined forces with calls to educate children in grit and expectations that one will fight to earn one's position and goods in a competitive marketplace.[40] Increasingly, being American is reduced to individual pursuit of the American Dream in terms of wealth and property, relinquishing *e pluribus unum*, common goods, and other collective ends historically valued in America. This focus on individuals and private success feeds a climate of distrust toward others who might get in our way, who may be after some of the same things we are, or who may jeopardize our personal interests.

Distrust may be helpful for a democracy to the extent that it can keep citizens on guard against tyranny. Additionally, minority members who've faced a history of being harmed may use distrust to rightfully protect themselves from reoccurring harm.[41] Moreover, minority members who lack economic resources tend to be more distrustful of others, in part because they have more to lose if others fail them or take advantage of them.[42] But today's environment has reached a troubling level of distrust across demographic groups. When people lack trust in others, collaborative effort is discouraged. They doubt others will act for the right reasons or on behalf of the common good. Moreover, they may feel others are not worthy of self-government and should be closely overseen by military or authoritarian leaders.

Relatedly, Americans increasingly do not trust each other to make wise political decisions. That distrust is magnified by growing political polarization and hyperpartisanship, with more citizens increasingly detesting their counterparts on the other side of the aisle, and calling them derogatory names like "libtards" or "deplorables."[43] And whereas a significant percentage once claimed to desire compromise between parties, only 46% of Democrats and 44% of Republicans do today.[44] This may be because citizens are increasingly encouraged to fight for their own advantage and not settle for middle ground.[45] Or, it may be because citizens are less willing to compromise with those believed to be unwise or untrustworthy.

The situation of distrust and refusal to compromise is exacerbated by citizens having little interaction across lines of difference. Experts in civil life explain,

> One reason that Americans trust each other less may be that they no longer engage in the large, connected civil associations that predominated in the twentieth century. Religious congregations and unions were two of the biggest components of civil society; together they drew an outright majority of American adults as recently as 1970. By 2012, they reached just one in three adults. Newspapers also played an integrating role, but their audience has fallen dramatically.[46]

Not only have rates of civil participation declined but also the composition of those groups has changed. A leading sociologist of democracy, Theda Skocpol claims that while "for decade after decade in U.S. civil life until recently, major voluntary associations involved considerable popular participation and mobilized people of different occupational and class backgrounds into the same or parallel groups," civil organizations are now more segregated by social class and lack a shared identity that historically united them across differences.[47] More recently, the most wealthy Americans organize using their clout and political ties, largely in terms of business and individual interests, almost entirely only with each other. Upper-middle-class professionals tend to work only with their similarly highly educated peers on social problems. And working-class people, historically involved in union work, have increasingly dropped out of civil society.[48] This situation of dwindling civil life is especially troublesome for rural people living in so-called civic deserts, which lack places to meet, ways to deliberate about issues, or opportunities to interact with people different from themselves—experiences that might aid in overcoming fear, resentment, and distrust.[49] As more people are unable or unwilling to participate in organizations that, in many instances, have demonstrated considerable impact on political and shared life, those people may feel less able to influence democracy today.

The isolation of citizens from each other and especially from those different from themselves contributes to the experience of democratic distance, a concept that Christopher LeBron draws from James Baldwin.[50] Even though we may share the land that is America, our physical location within the same country is not enough to bind us as countrymen, for our experiences of reality within that space are often quite different—we are distant from each other when it comes to our experience of democracy. A black man, for example, experiences far more checks on his freedom, as he faces greater likelihood of being pulled over by police when driving, greater chances of being shot by police, or greater prison sentences when found guilty of the same crime as a white man. As a result, blacks and whites have very different experiences of freedom in America and such differences magnify the gaps between us, leading to distrust for those whose experiences and claims seem so radically different from our own.[51] And it leads blacks to be rightfully distrustful of and angered by the hypocrisy of whites who proclaim freedom and other ideals in America yet fail to recognize how those are not carried out equitably across our land.

Trust does not fare any better when it comes to trusting politicians. A majority of Americans now say they distrust elected public officials, especially at the federal level.[52] In part, this distrust has been driven by bad governance and political scandals. But distrust is also magnified as populations age, become less financially stable, and consume more media.[53] As a result, some older citizens may now feel that strong authoritarian leaders they find trustworthy are needed to rule over our changing country.

Often those Americans who have not been successful in the past, or do not see viable avenues for being so in the future, fatalistically accept these conditions of inequity, distrust, and divisiveness. They become passive about countering or changing them, resigning themselves to the way the world is. Whereas, I will explain, hope asserts that the world can be changed and even improved. Other Americans, often those who have enough resources and power to be comfortable with the present conditions, indulge in the privilege of being cynical or apathetic. Sometimes one's position of relative comfort leads one to disregard calls to improve the lives of others, writing them off with a simple "that doesn't affect me."[54] Often cynicism functions like an armor one uses to shield oneself from risk or danger. Cynics quickly discount proposals for change or improvement, grumbling "why bother?" or "there's no way that's going to work." Thereby, they protect themselves from the effort those proposals might require and the potential harm they might bring. It is safe to be cynical, whereas hope entails risk—a proclivity toward possibility whose outcomes are unknown or unsure. Yet, even as cynicism may protect one from having to care about or engage in real effort and the problems that may result, it also relinquishes one's ability to even do so. For when we are cynical and believe that there's nothing we can do to make a difference, we hand over our power.

The collective action of hope also often requires venturing into areas of uncertainty. Sometimes naysayers focus on those uncertainties and breed distrust of leaders in social and political movements so that forward momentum stalls. Some spread states of hopelessness or jaded negativity through memes and messages on social media, especially skepticism about the role and effectiveness of government.[55] Cynics, believing that their political efforts are useless or ineffective and perhaps that everyone acts in self-interest, are left to look out merely for themselves, without a sense of responsibility to act on behalf of others. Indeed, cynics may mock others who do not hold such views as naïve and out of touch with reality. Cynicism functions as a distancing maneuver, separating citizens from each other, from democratic institutions, and from civil organizations, where visions of an improved world and action to achieve it tend to occur.

In America, loneliness and social isolation are increasingly widespread, on the rise, and the worst for members of Generation Z, born between the mid-1990s and the early 2000s.[56] Loneliness can lead one to feel disconnected from others and disengaged from political life. Additionally, loneliness and isolation seem to relate to political perceptions. For example, of Millennials described as "lost and disengaged," many feel unprepared for and unsure of how to participate in political life, leaving them feeling less confident than the roughly half of Americans who believe that citizens can influence political life.[57] My notion of hope aims to span those divides between people and to overcome cynicism, while building belief in the efficacy of civil and political engagement.

Privatized Hope

Finally, what is left of hope has become privatized.[58] This phenomenon is exacerbated as neoliberalism continues to assert Margaret Thatcher's claims, "There is no such thing as society, only individuals and families," and "there is no alternative to the market." Hope is reduced to a mere drive to achieve one's own limited dreams, typically only through financial terms and material goods, such as a salesman hoping that he earns the end-of-year bonus for highest sales of the year so he can buy a fancy new sedan as a sign of his success to others. Sometimes such achievements are seen as a zero-sum game, where our personal success is threatened by other citizens or immigrants who appear to be competing for our desired goods, position, or power, leading us to be further distrustful of them. And, as we focus on our personal desires, we may lose sight of public goods that benefit all citizens as well as our collective avenues for fulfilling them.

When citizens are rendered isolated competitors, they lose the ability to detect social problems and the motivation to ameliorate them, especially if the effects on one's self or family are not immediate. One economist describes some of these citizens as the new "complacent class," who are content with the way things are as long as they are not directly harmed and as long as they can stay surrounded by people and things that confirm their experience of the world. We see this demonstrated in the rise of hyperpartisan confirmation bias and echo chambers, where those citizens only turn to others like themselves to confirm their beliefs. In their complacency, the members of the complacent class are unable to "inspire an electorate with any kind of strong positive visions, other than some marginal adjustments."[59] I aim to show how hope is better understood and enacted as a social and political endeavor that brings us into contact with an array of others as we craft substantially improved visions of the future, many of which depend on first identifying and solving social problems.

In sum, these changes in citizens' lives and views debilitate individuals and democracy as a whole. They keep us from recognizing and addressing collective problems and from leading better lives together. Citizens sit around waiting for reasons to hope, sometimes becoming swept up in campaign rhetoric when election cycles come around, unable or unwilling to see that hope is generated through action as citizens working together. Moreover, these conditions and their causes contribute to the seeming opposite of hope: despair. When we are in despair, we aren't sure how to move forward. We feel disconnected from our goals and from the agency we need to pursue them. We also tend to feel disconnected from other people, which is significant because those other people might help us craft our goals or provide us means for achieving them. This sense of isolation blocks the solidarity with others often needed to fulfill our aims.[60]

In addition to our personal struggles, political despair grows when we don't see enough political will or action to address major public problems. This leads us to doubt our ability to solve problems and may actually undermine our ability to do so. We may come to feel that our social problems are so great that we cannot possibly tackle them or even influence them. Indeed, there is some basis for such feeling, because data shows that individuals without significant wealth and resources are far less likely to influence government and its leaders.[61] For those knowledgeable of or sensing this inequity, their political despair played out through withdrawal from political life reflects more than just cynicism or apathy.[62] Finally, political despair can tempt citizens to give up on their commitment to justice, freedom, and better living for themselves and others.[63] As a result, authoritarianism and other forms of governmental rule may seem more appealing. When many Americans forgo those commitments, our social order and long-standing values may be undermined. Hence, we must overcome despair to revive and improve democracy today.

Moving Forward

In this book, I aim to articulate what hope is, why it matters to democracy, and how we should cultivate it. Rather than seeing hope as a mere personal emotion or tied to faith in God, I situate hope in explicitly political realms by considering the role hope plays in democracy and how it might be fostered in schools and civil society. Speaking to concerned and struggling citizens on both sides of the aisle, as well as educators working to develop good citizens, I intend to offer philosophically grounded yet accessible insight into our current state of affairs and suggestions for improvement. I will propose how we might move forward together to build hope—not a particular program of political action, but a way of life that can help to support democracy in general.

I come to this project as a white, Midwest farmer's daughter who retains the communal hard work ethic of family farming and the value of civic participation of my youth. My worldview was broadened as I left the farm for college, married a man in the military who served during a contentious period of war, experienced divorce and remarriage, and spent considerable time living and traveling abroad. I am now a well-educated, middle-aged adult living in a large city, and my political affiliation has shifted from Right to Left. Across that span of time and ideology, my life has been relatively privileged. Despite encountering some personal hardship, facing sexism, and witnessing the political frustration and economic struggles of my rural and less-educated family members, I have not experienced the significant or lasting oppression, racism, and injustice of the sort that has led many other citizens to despair. Certainly, the arguments I make in this book are influenced by this positionality. But they are also shaped by the hope I have cultivated, including a proclivity to see opportunities to work across divisions and to envision better futures ahead for social and political life in America. I realize the case I make will be a hard sell to some of you, and, indeed, I have much to learn from the questions and challenges you pose. Nonetheless, I invite you to join me in exploring such hope in the chapters to come.

In the next chapter, I begin by revealing some of the problematic ways in which hope has been understood. I consider one of those problematic forms of hope, grit, in much more detail later in the book. I then turn to the tradition of American pragmatism to construct an alternative account of hope that arises out of our American history and addresses our struggles today. In the third chapter, I detail how hope works as a set of pragmatist habits, a unique understanding of identity and proclivities to take action. In chapter 4, I explain how habits of hope can sustain and improve democracy, while at the same time, democracy can provide conditions that support hope. I describe both the content of what we might hope for in a democracy and the process of how we hope together. I show how each shapes our identity as Americans.

But hope is more than just a political project, it is also an educational one. In chapters 5 and 6, I look at how we can cultivate hope formally through education and informally in our lives together. I critique increasingly popular calls to teach grit, which may seem to be related to hope, but raise serious problems for us as individuals and as a democratic society. Instead, I locate learning how to hope within citizenship education that builds student agency, crafts new stories about America and the future we desire, and engages in dissent and other forms of effort to put forward alternative ways of living. I primarily describe teaching how to hope within the K-12 context, a context in which education is compulsory and many of our ways of interacting with others are still relatively malleable. But many of my proposals can be extended into college classrooms, and some are developmentally appropriate there. I use "teacher," "school," and "student" such that, in most instances, they might also refer to "professor," "university," and "learner of any age." Throughout the book, I describe a way of hoping together that may better support democratic life in these challenging times, and may be adapted for the unknown future of our country.

2

Looking Back to Move Forward

Our country is struggling with political despair, cynicism, and fatalism. Some citizens feel left behind and others feel powerless to improve their conditions through democratic means. Democracy stands on shaky ground; as wary citizens grow increasingly distrustful of elected officials and their fellow citizens, they turn to authoritarian alternatives. Citizens may be wondering, "How can I hope?" In response to those conditions, I offer an account of how citizens can hope that arises out of American history and our more than two centuries of democratic experimentation. This chapter lays the initial framework for that account in pragmatist philosophy, a philosophical tradition that developed in the United States in the late twentieth-century and has experienced a recent resurgence in America and abroad. That framework will then be pieced together into a more comprehensive description of hope in the next chapter. For those who are less familiar with philosophy, bear with me through this chapter, as I try to present key philosophical ideas in an accessible way, though recognize it can still be challenging to wrap one's head around. I believe it will be worth your while, for I contend that this pragmatist version of hope is robust enough to sustain us through challenging times and support us as we craft a better American future.

Common and Limited Understandings of Hope

In order to distinguish the unique character of pragmatist hope and its usefulness for addressing current struggles in America, it's worthwhile to first clarify the ways in which hope is more commonly understood. Doing so offers a useful foil for revealing key differences and highlighting what pragmatism has to offer. It's important to recognize that empirical research shows that hope is actually experienced and enacted differently among various populations, drawing on different combinations of affective, cognitive, and behavioral dimensions. In other words, people hope differently, with varying beliefs, emotions, and actions. These differences suggest that hope is socially

Learning How to Hope. Sarah M. Stitzlein, Oxford University Press (2020). © Oxford University Press.
DOI: 10.1093/oso/9780190062651.001.0001

mediated; we shape it by our cultural norms and local practices. As such, hope is capable of being influenced by environment and education.[64]

The first and most significant (mis)conception of hope is that it is often described in individualist terms. It is confined to the feelings, beliefs, or actions of one person, which often play out internally or without impact on others. Hope is only about one person's anticipation, desires, and efforts. This individualist understanding fails to encapsulate the full process of hoping and its potential impact on shared living—elements central to improving our civil and political lives that I will address in the following chapters.

Some people refer to hope as an emotion, a feeling an individual has that motivates her to have a certain outlook on the world. A marathon runner, like me, may think, "I hope to win my next race." That hope entails a feeling of excitement, nervousness, and anticipation within her as she pictures receiving her medal or listening to people cheer as she crosses the finish. As a result, she arrives at the starting line feeling excited and ready to take on the challenge. Yet, many of us also recognize a cognitive element to hope. The cognitive aspects work in coordination with our emotions to help us make calculations about what is likely to happen in a situation and how we can influence the outcome. As we calculate outcomes, we may feel exhilaration and expectancy. Indeed, psychologists have identified the elevated feeling one experiences when surveying the environment and projecting a better future ahead.[65] So, as the marathon runner prepares for the big race, she may think carefully about how far and how fast she should run during her training in order to enhance the possibility of winning the race. She may reflect on the outcomes of prior races and the successes of her competitors to determine whether her chances of winning are good. It is those rational deliberations combined with her emotions that bring her to the starting line confident for the race to begin.

Philosophers have encapsulated this phenomenon within their orthodox definition of hope as desire in the face of uncertainty. They argue that hope is a combination of desire and belief, where one desires a specific outcome, but is uncertain about whether it may be obtained. These desires are for things that we really want to occur or be fulfilled, but are sufficiently uncertain, such that we cannot count or plan on them. This belief-desire model of hope entails both beliefs about what is possible and a reflection of what we value or want.[66] This believing, desiring, and feeling largely happens within one's self. So, even if that marathon runner has won many marathons in the past and she wants to continue her streak, it is uncertain that she will do so. A new and faster runner may have entered the race or the runner may trip and injure herself midway through, possibilities that keep her from counting on winning even as she is overcome with desire for doing so.

Psychologists, especially those working in the subfield of positive psychology and those studying the educational idea of grit, also point inward to describe hope as an approach to fulfilling clearly stated goals. Positive psychologists focus on helping people achieve happy and flourishing lives. They claim that hope is an individual's use of willpower, a form of mental energy that propels one toward one's objectives, and "waypower," a mental capacity to chart a course to those objectives.[67] Hope, then, drives one's individual actions and is a way of performing our own agency. While they may ultimately be concerned with human happiness, positive psychologists tend to not take into account the actual outcomes of one's deeds, focusing instead on just the practice of hope.

Sometimes, those individuals then pursue their own goals with little concern for their impact on other people and sometimes without even rationally acknowledging the constraints of reality. This is too often the case with the much-celebrated idea of grit that is sweeping our schools as a new educational aim, which I address in chapter 5. Returning to the marathon example, a marathon runner may become so fixed on seeing herself as an elite distance athlete that she overlooks or even disregards the impact that extensive hours of training have on the well-being of her young child and husband who depend on her for companionship. While her willpower and waypower may pave the way toward athletic success, they may harm her relationships or deprive her family members of the attention they need to thrive.

Hope is also often invoked in religious contexts. Theologians tend to locate hope in an individual's faith in a deity who will act on his or her behalf.[68] The desire for a better future, perhaps even a glorious afterlife, is then allocated based on the faith, belief, and/or practices of the individual, depending on his religious affiliation.[69] Or, theologians focus on the power of god(s), thereby potentially belittling our agency and leading us to be passive as we wait for god(s) to act. Some theologians and philosophers distinguish ultimate hopes that are focused on particular objectives, like winning a race, from fundamental or absolute hope, which is a more open-ended outlook about the future or the enduring goodness of God. Perhaps we might think of this as a more general spirit of hopefulness.[70]

Sometimes hope is confused with other phenomena, such as wishing or planning. When calculating the outcomes of achieving a goal, if the likelihood is very high or near certain, then it doesn't make sense to hope for it; rather, one may merely plan on it occurring. If the likelihood is extremely low or when we cannot identify means to achieve our desired ends, then hope is also not the appropriate response; instead, one may engage in wishful thinking. Wishful thinking is more passive, while hoping is an active orientation toward identifying feasible goals, constructing a narrative for why they are valuable, justifying how one will continue to pursue them in the face of obstacles, and actively chasing them.[71]

Sometimes hope is confused with optimism, in part because both are focused on better possibilities in the future. Indeed, many people commonly use the words interchangeably, but their meanings should be distinguished. Like wishful thinking, optimism is passive, certain, and complacent. It holds that things will work out for the best, regardless of our interventions. Sometimes dubbed "blind optimism," it functions as such in that it keeps one from fully seeing reality, including long-standing or significant obstacles that stand in the way of one's desired future. This distorted view of reality can lead one to deceive oneself about what is feasible for one's future. Such optimism then becomes cruel when one can never quite fulfill that vision that seemed so certain.[72] Hope, however, carefully accounts for those obstacles in one's rational deliberations, tempering one's predictions, and recognizing harmful myths that may disguise or perpetuate injustice.[73] It is an active, though uncertain and sometimes discontent, orientation to life and its struggles.

While the theologians direct our attention to deities and psychologists emphasize that we should hope regardless of real-world constraints or problematic implications for others, pragmatist hope, as I will show, is firmly rooted in the real circumstances of life on Earth. Rather than a religious faith, which entails an adherence to God or ideology, pragmatists exhibit faith by being willing to try out ideas and to pursue desired ends even in the face of uncertainty or difficulty. It is a form of courage in human ingenuity and risk taking.[74] While many philosophers, psychologists, and theologians describe hope in individualist terms, a pragmatist notion of hope works to encompass the larger social process of hoping. It connects individuals to other people and can be used not only to pursue our individual goals but also to enrich our experiences in communities and our larger outlook on life in a democracy. Because it is rooted in the real circumstances of our lives, it cannot be disconnected from social and political life.[75] Moreover, pragmatist hope can help us to better face current political struggles and social problems, all the while building a democratic identity together.[76]

Pragmatism, Democracy, and America

It comes as no surprise that hope is a key part of pragmatism given that this philosophical perspective arose largely in the late 1800s in America—a land founded and sustained on hope. While pragmatists were writing in France, Italy, and England by the early 1900s, pragmatism seems to align with the American spirit, if such a thing can be captured. Pragmatism emphasizes facing difficult conditions and responding with inquiry to understand them, ingenuity to experiment with improving them, and vision to craft a better future. Its roots trace to the American revolution, where an outlook of experimentation and dissent was taking hold in our new country. Historian William Goetzmann points to Thomas Paine, who arrived in America and magnified its budding personality. "According to Paine, America was God's country of the future. The spirit of revival, constant regeneration, and future-oriented habits of pragmatic thinking had already become basic to American thought. Paine, as myth-maker, used it to build an intercolonial self-identity intended to bind the colonies together in a common cause and a new utopian nation."[77] In the image of Paine, being an American meant building social and political life anew, breaking away from old routines and their injustices, and seeking to create new and freer ways of living.

On his heels, Ralph Waldo Emerson described America as an event that was unfolding in accordance with the visions and actions of its citizens, rather than long-standing foundations of church or nature.[78] Emerson believed that the future of America could be better through people shaping and enacting democracy together—a message that later hit home with twentieth-century pragmatist John Dewey, who called Emerson "the Philosopher of Democracy."[79] Indeed, Emerson's focus on possibility and human agency, without need for firm foundations, seems to have also impacted Dewey's classic pragmatist peers Charles Sanders Peirce and William James.[80] That uncertain and vague future, dependent on our actions, led Americans to invoke hope as they searched for the best ways to create and sustain freedom.[81] In reaction to the Civil War, many Americans sought reconciliation by rejecting divisiveness in favor of a more open and experimental worldview; pragmatism fit the bill. Its embrace of science and change also aligned well with the development of new technology and industry across the country. Pragmatism complemented the late nineteenth- and early twentieth-century mainstream social imaginary—how we understood ourselves, our relation to each other, and our role in the world. But, importantly, pragmatism also was not a simple form of idealism; instead, it focused on real constraints. Even as it celebrated human agency and efforts to improve the world, pragmatism calls us to recognize that agency and effort have long been restricted due to factors such as one's social position as a member of a racial minority or one's lack of economic and cultural resources.[82]

Walt Whitman, whom Dewey dubbed the seer of democracy, also influenced the classic pragmatists.[83] Whitman celebrated America because of what it might become and noted our responsibilities to one another as we shape that future together. Whitman's poetry, which put forward visions of what might be, sparked action. Some pragmatists, like James, followed Whitman's aesthetic approaches to breaking down simplistic dualisms that cast people and things in clearly competing categories without the complexity needed to fully understand or transform them. Others, including much more recent American pragmatists like Richard Rorty, picked up on a sense of social hope operating in Whitman.[84] Whitman looked to the future, the consequences of one's actions, and the ideals shaping them to assess their worthiness.

While pragmatists generally followed this formula as they developed their theory of truth, their focus on the future also led to discontent. In other words, seeing that the present world did not stack up to the visions they had in mind, they were led to criticize the status quo and generate new possibilities. American historical essayist Louis Menand explains, "Pragmatism belongs to a disestablishmentarian impulse in American culture—an impulse that drew strength from the writings of Emerson, who attacked institutions and conformity, and from the ascendancy, after the Civil War, of evolutionary theories, which drew attention to the contingency of all social forms."[85] Pragmatism perpetuated the spirit of dissent in the American Founders, encouraging citizens to speak out against unsatisfactory conditions and put forward alternatives. Progressive Era pragmatists later turned the romance of Emerson and the aesthetics of Whitman into a way of life entailing dissent, vision, creation, and action—a burgeoning form of hope.

Pragmatism fell relatively silent in the mid-1900s, as new forms of analytic philosophy took hold. Moreover, the social imaginary of the country was challenged and reshaped, as American optimism was shattered in the face of the atrocities of World War II and Vietnam abroad and racism at home. Following World War II and into the Cold War, some social leaders feared the ramifications of a philosophical practice seen as subversive and activist. At a time when stability and authority were desired, the contingent experimentation of pragmatism appeared dangerous to some.[86] As those fears declined in the late twentieth century and new thinkers gained the spotlight, pragmatism once again came to the fore, spurred by the work of a few key scholars whom I describe later in this book.

Contemporary pragmatist Colin Koopman rightly concludes, "If pragmatism is American, this is because America, like pragmatism, is an emblematic vision of hope. Pragmatism is thus best understood as a philosophical practice corollary to the experiment of American democracy."[87] While that's not to say that all Americans are hopeful or that hope has been consistently present in America, pragmatism has worked hand-in-hand with hope as a lasting and significant part of our history and national identity.

Key Elements of Pragmatism

Paradoxically, pragmatism has a lot to communicate about hope yet pragmatists actually have said very little about it. While it may seem odd to write a book on hope using philosophers who have not actually said much about it, hope is integral to pragmatism. But, many key pragmatists, especially classic pragmatists of the late nineteenth and early twentieth centuries, have not discussed hope explicitly or in depth. Inklings of hope can be traced most significantly to John Dewey and appear more recently and more explicitly within the work of Richard Rorty, Judith Green, Patrick Shade, Colin Koopman, Robert Westbrook, and Cornel West. Of the contemporary pragmatists writing in the late twentieth and early twenty-first centuries who have more directly considered hope, most have not extended their work on hope to implications for democracy or education, as I do in this book. I build my pragmatist account of hope largely on the philosophy of John Dewey. Notably, Dewey himself does not provide explicit details about hope, even though it underlies much of his work. It was also evident in his own personal and political life as he dealt with the loss of two of his children and his wife, while also facing two world wars and speaking out about the harmful democratic implications of consolidating power among wealthy industrialists.

Hope arises out of central elements of pragmatism, including pragmatism's notions of inquiry, growth, truth, meliorism, and habits, which I detail in the following sections. I aim to make these philosophically dense concepts more accessible to the reader, as they are important for shedding light on a rich notion of hope. Through this chapter and the next, I will show how the spirit and approach of pragmatism reflects and enhances everyday life in our country historically and today. Unlike other philosophical traditions, pragmatism is focused on sustaining and improving civil life. It is not merely a way of thinking about the world, but a call to engagement in civil and political life. In this regard, it is well suited for the current needs of our struggling democracy.

Though it is often implicit within pragmatist writings, I will tease out a pragmatist account of hope as a set of habits that lead one to act to improve one's life and, often, the lives of others. Pragmatist hope recognizes the difficulty of current circumstances, but approaches them with thoughtful action, effort, and belief that things can be improved. That is not to say that there are not significant differences among the views of pragmatists, but I focus largely here on what unites them in their understanding of hope. Like Koopman, "I understand pragmatism, and find it at its best, as a philosophical way of taking hope seriously. Pragmatism develops the philosophical resources of hope."[88]

Inquiry

Early pragmatist Charles Sanders Peirce limits his discussions of hope largely to his description of inquiry—the way we come to know, question, and improve the world and ourselves. Inquiry is the process through which we investigate the world around us, hypothesize improved understandings or ways of living, and then experiment with them. Hope is a condition that leads us to believe that inquiry is worthwhile and will contribute to new ideas. It helps us to view the world as intelligible to us. For without hope that our questions can be answered, we may never initiate inquiry.[89] And we must have hope in order to view the slow progress of scientific inquiry and experimentation as eventually yielding useful results.

Peirce describes hope as a sentiment and yet celebrates its role in logical thinking.[90] He says,

We are, doubtless, in the main logical animals, but we are not perfectly so. Most of us, for example, are naturally more sanguine and hopeful than logic would justify. We seem to be so constituted that in the absence of any facts to go upon we are happy and self-satisfied; so that the effect of experience is continually to contract our hopes and aspirations. Yet a lifetime of the application of this corrective does not usually eradicate our sanguine disposition. Where hope is unchecked by any experience, it is likely that our optimism is extravagant. Logicality in regard to practical matters is the most useful quality an animal can possess, and might, therefore, result from the action of natural selection.[91]

Elizabeth Cooke rightfully interprets this passage to show that hope alone is not enough, but rather its value depends on how well it is informed by experience and not simply wishful thinking. And, while hope is not rational for Peirce, it is an impulse that can be put to good use to urge us forward in inquiry. Hope is useful because it predisposes us to inquiry and to the testing of ideas in experience. It works, in part through imagination and hypothesis formation, to come up with ideas that extend beyond the current state of affairs or what we know.

For Dewey, hope sometimes arises within the midst of despair, when we have lost our way and are struggling to move forward. We may feel powerless because we aren't sure how to get ourselves unstuck or don't feel able to do so. Dewey describes these moments as "indeterminate situations." He turns to the process of inquiry via the empirical method to help us explore those situations, consider possible courses of action, and test out various solutions. It is inquiry that helps us to understand, act on, and reconstruct our environments and our experiences so that we are able to move forward out of the indeterminate situation. In a richly cognitive and often social practice, inquiry invokes curiosity and problem-solving to move us out of ruts. Indeed, this method combats the stagnation of fatalism by urging us to formulate and test solutions, often alongside others facing similar problems.

Classical pragmatists were committed to scientific inquiry and empirical experimentation, held open to revision through fallibilism, the belief that truth claims could never be certain and were subject to human error. Shared inquiry is a way to solve problems, whether they be personal or social, and a way of living democratically together, thereby further tying together pragmatism with the goals of early America. Deweyan inquiry is well aligned with democracy because it is experimental in nature and invites multiple, and often conflicting, perspectives into deliberation with each other to choose or design a path forward. Within inquiry, the focus is less on what we can know for certain and more on how we can learn and change both our world and ourselves. Classical pragmatists were especially interested in habits as the key platform for such learning and changing, which I will say more about in the next chapter.

Growth

We grow when we apply what we learn from inquiry into indeterminate situations and create ways to reestablish smooth living that carries us from one activity to the next. As a result of our inquiries, we may discover the need to change our environments or ourselves. Doing so develops physical, intellectual, and moral capacities as we reflect on our needs and those of others around us. Many people wrongly assume, however, that growth necessarily has an end—as if it were "movement toward a fixed goal."[92] We tend to think of growth as only progression toward some specific outcome, such as mastering bicycle riding or graduating from high school. But this way of thinking tends to place the emphasis on the static terminus, rather than focusing on the process of growing as itself educative and worthwhile.

Dewey's alternative view of growth does not neatly and linearly move toward a fixed goal, perhaps like the ideal "waypower" of some positive psychologists noted earlier. Instead, he describes trajectories that are more complicated, often shifting with the environment. Moreover, holding onto a fixed goal may be undesirable because doing so employs a limited or possibly foreclosed vision of the future. We cannot know the future with certainty, nor do we want to limit ourselves to what is merely likely in the future, so our ultimate goals must remain flexible and open. Instead, as changes occur in the environment, Dewey asserts that people must continually inquire into moments of uncertainty and novel circumstances, develop new hypotheses about those situations, and revise their aims.

Dewey works with what he calls "ends-in-view," which are relatively close and feasible, even if difficult to achieve, rather than overarching goals at some final endpoint in the future. Often, the ends we hope for are some improvement on our current state of affairs, but their pursuit also nurtures our abilities, leading us to value both the end and the means we acquire or employ for achieving it. Those ends-in-view guide our decisions and hypotheses along the way, keeping us resourceful and attuned to present circumstances and the opportunities they present so that we can move toward that desired alternative. That includes recognizing the intrinsic value of the present means to our ends-in-view, which help us to experience fulfillment in the present.[93] And it includes valuing the larger disposition toward the future and its possibilities that can help to move us forward in the present through challenging times.

Each fulfilled end-in-view sustains our hope by highlighting meaningful headway and directing our further action. Ends-in-view later become means to future ends, working in an ongoing continuum. This sustenance of hope differs from theological accounts, which are difficult to sustain on faith alone, and may leave believers frustrated at an apparent lack of improvement. It also differs from positive psychology and grit literature, which tend to focus on large, far-off, and challenging goals that one holds tenaciously.

Many people think of hope as goal-directed and future-oriented. While objects of hope for pragmatists may temporarily serve as ends-in-view, the practice of hope moves us forward through inquiry and experimentation as we pursue our complicated trajectory. It helps to unify our past, present, and future. Hope, then, is not just about a vision of the future, but rather a way of living purposively in the present that is informed by the past and what is anticipated to come. Sometimes we recognize that people and conditions in our past have supported us as we grow, thereby leading us to appreciate those historical influences and to seek to preserve them in our communities, our actions, and ourselves.[94] The past offers us patterns, examples, and stories of previous successes that can help us shape our present actions. And looking back at history reminds us that the world was different and that the future, too, can be different.[95] Whereas utopian views of what could be may actually immobilize and exhaust one in the present because they are overwhelming, pragmatist hope is always tied to what one *is* doing and feasibly *can do* in the present, especially when equipped with knowledge of the past. Such continuity prevents us from being swept up in wishful thinking, where ends do not arise out of past and present, and means for achieving the desired future are out of reach.[96]

Dewey's ends-in-view process of growth sheds some light onto how pragmatist hope offers a blending of ultimate hope (having specific objectives) and fundamental hope (a general orientation to the future). Ends-in-view give us revisable and flexible goals, but the process of growth is more concerned with our disposition toward the future and its open-endedness as we encounter unpredictability and make our way through indeterminate situations. Goal-focused and overarching hopes may reinforce one another as we connect our past experiences and move into the future, with all of its unpredictability. Whereas despair limits us, hope supports growth. Summarizing Dewey's account of growth and its related contributions to hope, Rorty concludes: "Hope—the ability to believe that the future will be unspecifiably different from, and unspecifiably freer than, the past—is the condition of growth."[97]

Truth

Peirce was the first to begin to articulate a pragmatist understanding of truth, offering a maxim that his followers picked up and expanded on: "Consider what effects, that might conceivably have practical bearings, we conceive the object of our conception to have. Then, our conception of these effects is the whole of our conception of the object."[98] While challenging to comprehend, Peirce is saying that when we are trying to determine whether an idea is true, we must look at its effects. We determine the truth of our idea based on its consequences. Central to pragmatist philosophy, ideas become true insofar as they "work" for us, fruitfully combine our experiences, and lead us to further experiences that satisfy our needs. Pragmatists are concerned with the concrete differences in our lived experiences that an idea's being true will make. In other words, they focus on the consequences of our ideas to see if they are useful or improve our lives.

We must consider how to grow and flourish alongside others as we craft our ends-in-view and determine what is truthful in the world. This differs considerably from other philosophical and psychological accounts of hope based on the desire of objects or states of affairs regardless of whether they are good for us or other people. Pragmatic truth expresses "the successful completing of a worthwhile leading."[99] Unlike more common views of truth as a corresponding match between proposition and reality, pragmatist truth is something that occurs when the goals of human flourishing are satisfied— at least temporarily. Built into these criteria is consideration of the well-being of others, for successful leading through experiences almost always requires working and communicating together. Determining truth connects us with others and can present opportunities to share struggles and bear witness to the suffering and successes of others. This is a significant component of pragmatism given that in today's society the suffering of people of color, immigrants, the poor, transgender people, and others is often hidden or ignored. Pragmatism pushes us to consider the well-being of others, urging us to shed light on their struggles and to attend to them in order to bring about greater flourishing for ourselves and others.

Additionally, the differences an idea will make are quite limited, and therefore less truthful, if relevant only to one person. Because of this, we must seek out the perspectives of and impact on others in order to verify truthfulness. Norms regarding equitable and just communication are entailed both in collecting evidence of the consequences of ideas on the lives of others and in deliberating about and determining their usefulness.[100]

Truth as "what works" is that which helps us navigate the world, avoid difficulties, and get out of problematic situations; it is what helps us and others to flourish. In James's words, "Truth *happens* to an idea" as we trace and determine its practical consequences, often through inquiry and experimentation that validates our hypotheses and experiences.[101] Like growth, truth brings together past, present, and future in that it does not merely repeat the past but rather renews it with innovations for the future so that fruitful living can be maintained.[102] That is to say, truth is not merely established once and for all and then carried through time, but rather many ideas must adapt and improve in order to remain truthful as a result of our ongoing assessments of their consequences. Pragmatists then base the content of their hopes on the findings of our inquiry, our knowledge of the past and present, and our predictions about the future. This typically keeps them realistic and feasible.

Yet the pragmatist accounts of growth and truth show that there can be beliefs that are worthwhile to hold even if they aren't based on evidence that bears out in empirical inquiry. For example, having hope for a cure or a better outcome as one faces a life-threatening illness may go against the evidence, yet such a view might still be worthwhile for living out a satisfactory life with a positive outlook on the world as a whole, rather than one plagued by suffering and negativity. Hence, while pragmatism is centrally concerned with evidence and experience that builds informed aims or ultimate hopes, pragmatist hope is open to exceeding the evidence, allowing a larger sense of fundamental hope, or hopefulness.

Unlike his predecessors who rarely mentioned hope, neopragmatist Rorty makes hope more explicit and uses it in a fairly radical way. His late twentieth-century writing ushered in a new generation of pragmatist commentary on and employment of the notion of hope. He introduces hope largely as a foil to the quest for truth that other nonpragmatist philosophers have supported—the belief that we can come to discover and know propositions that reflect a real, objective reality. He said, "substituting hope for knowledge, substituting the idea that the ability to be citizens of the full-fledged democracy which is yet to come, rather than the ability to grasp truth, is what is important about being human."[103] So, rather than pursuing truth, which can be an unengaging endeavor to objectively determine reality, Rorty insists on the more radical project of aiming for hope in America. This is, in part, because, like earlier pragmatists, he values beliefs insofar as they are useful to us and he sees beliefs based in narratives of hope as especially useful for shaping our lives. Those narratives include everything from novels to journalism to ethnographies. Those narratives are based in the contingency of human lives and experiences, often providing descriptions of past suffering, an opportunity to build solidarity with others, and a vision of an improved future.

The narrative is "an attempt to interpret the situation of the oppressed group to the rest of their society. Such narratives increase human solidarity by expanding the sympathies of persons who are not members of the oppressed group so that they come to see the oppressed 'as one of us rather than as a them.'"[104] This makes it harder to marginalize people and easier to see solidarity with them. Moreover, we come to see, through the study of history, that we have shaped our community, and therefore can continue to have influence over it. Or, in Rorty's words, "Our identification with our community—our society, our political tradition, our intellectual heritage—is heightened when we see this community as *ours* rather than *nature's, shaped* rather than *found*, one among many which men have made."[105] Narratives can be used to guide our efforts through employing courage and imaginative experimentation, perhaps more boldly than suggested by some of his pragmatist colleagues.

Like Rorty, contemporary pragmatist Judith Green relinquishes what Dewey called, "the quest for certainty," yet she does not go as far as Rorty in replacing truth with hope entirely. Instead, she champions "a democratic social epistemology."[106] In this regard, Green reflects a more traditional pragmatist account of truth where people determine what works for them together by taking into account their varied experiences with an idea or situation. Green believes that Rorty focuses too much on hopeful narratives that provide solidarity among Americans and a vision of better American life. She contends that his stories tend to too quickly dissolve real harms and injustices experienced by some groups of Americans at the hands of others into a new common story.

Instead, Green follows the tragic optimism of Viktor Frankl and James Baldwin, where one's outlook for the future is informed by the harms dealt and endured in the past.[107] Her hope is grounded in the widespread suffering of multiple groups of people and relies on unifying them in working toward a better future that is informed by the harmful past. She then issues a call to her pragmatist peers to be public philosophers who support and embody democratic social hope. For Green, social hope arises out of experience, endures struggles, brings feelings of safety, and entails creative imagination. Social hope involves being concerned for and engaged with others. Green believes today's circumstances require not just the national call for hope that Rorty voiced, but a global vision of deeply democratic living. This is because when one group (America) puts its efforts toward hope without regarding the hopeful visions of other people, anti-American frustration grows, perpetuating cycles of hatred and fear.[108] Green concludes, "storytelling is a process of moving from fear and loss to vision and hope—a process through which many of us as individuals and all of us as people still must pass in order to bring us to the stage of readiness for cooperative, democracy-deepening transformative action."[109]

Meliorism

Classical pragmatists upheld meliorism, key to the notion of hope, as, in Dewey's words, "the idea that at least there is a sufficient basis of goodness in life and its conditions so that by thought and earnest effort we may constantly make things better."[110] Indeed, when looking at history, we see that America has become more just and freer over time, despite our past and present problems, such as continued racism and sexism, and despite the ways in which injustice has become less visible.[111] For example, while the end of slavery may be a primary example to celebrate, many African Americans remain subject to incarcerated labor that exploits them, though largely behind prison walls and unbeknownst to many Americans. I also recognize that while slavery may have ended, many African Americans continue to live in fear of having their bodies and lives unfairly claimed by police and others wielding societal power. There are certainly significant exceptions to the overall trend toward progress, and progress has not been achieved or distributed equitably to all. Nor has progress itself been constant, for we have faced setbacks and have moved forward in fits and starts. But the opportunity to work to improve the world is nearly always present.

Readers may share skepticism regarding my claim of progress,[112] but I contend the evidence is there to demonstrate improvement, especially improvement that has been hard won by advocates and activists for change.[113]

My life, for example, is freer than it likely would have been a century or more ago. As a result of the efforts of suffragists, I have the opportunity to vote as a woman, even though my state may currently engage in practices that suppress my ability to do so. Unlike early American educators who were banned or socially shunned, I also have the ability to work as a teacher outside of the home while a married mother, even though I may encounter some backlash from a portion of my family and friends who believe I should stay home with my young child. My claim of progress is not meant to suggest that the struggle is over or that justice is complete, nor is it blind to backslides, new forms of injustice that arise over time, or serious and destructive setbacks—even catastrophes—that lay well beyond the reach or influence of people, such as natural disasters that may exacerbate problems in our social and political lives. But I am saying that there is significant evidence to show us that we can make life better. Importantly, though, the conversation about progress should not stop there—with evidence of more or improved outcomes—but rather should ask challenging questions about the future we desire and what changes would count and for whom in order for us to declare progress achieved.[114] This is, in part, where the role of hope comes in, providing us a vision and criteria for determining its successful fulfillment. Hope provides us a direction and a rationale to guide our actions and is grounded in the belief that progress is possible.

Elected leaders, political movements, civil groups, and, importantly, everyday folks have all played a vital role in shaping that trajectory of increasing justice and freedom.[115] Unlike simple optimists, however, pragmatists do not hold that the situation will necessarily work out for the best, but rather they believe people should make efforts to contribute to better outcomes. In the words of contemporary pragmatist Cornel West, "Optimism adopts the role of the spectator who surveys the evidence in order to infer that things are going to get better. Yet when we know that the evidence does not look good . . . Hope enacts the stance of the participant who actively struggles against the evidence."[116] Dewey similarly explains that it would be foolish to believe that there is "an automatic and wholesale progress in human affairs," insisting instead that betterment "depends upon deliberative human foresight and socially constructive work."[117]

Pragmatism acknowledges the complexities and challenges of our circumstances, yet aims to approach them practically, with intelligent inquiry and thoughtful action, believing that those conditions can be improved.[118] It does not believe in inevitable progress, but rather looks at historical evidence to conclude that there has been a long record of struggle and possibility that reveals the past successes of others who responded with effort and suggests significant likelihood of potential success in the future, though recognizing that it is not guaranteed. The efforts invoked by meliorism are rarely undertaken alone; instead they are typically tied to others who are working together to solve problems. Meliorism is not merely the effort of individuals maintaining the status quo as they seek to improve their own lives, but rather that of civil and political groups, as well as individuals, who work to ameliorate injustice, hardship, and serious social problems.[119] The current of meliorism and its call to collective action runs strongest in the work of Dewey. Robert Westbrook goes so far as to call it "radically democratic meliorism."[120] As such, I draw most heavily on Dewey as I integrate meliorism into my account of pragmatist hope.

Pragmatism is also not aligned with pessimism, insofar as pragmatism asserts the possibility of improving our world and our experiences in it, rather than accepting those conditions as fixed or effort as futile. Because the optimist believes the situation will necessarily work out for the best so effort is unnecessary and the pessimist believes that intervention is futile and the outcome is doomed, both optimism and pessimism can be paralyzing. Meliorism, however, stimulates action in order to fulfill the possibility of bettering the world.[121]

The words of Martin Luther King Jr., a champion and practitioner of hope, were enshrined on the rug in Obama's oval office: "The arc of the moral universe is long, but it bends toward justice."[122] King later explained in a pragmatist spirit of meliorism, "Human progress never rolls on wheels of inevitability; it comes through the tireless efforts of men willing to be coworkers with God, and without this hard work, time itself becomes an ally of the forces of social stagnation. We must use time creatively, in the knowledge that the time is always ripe to do right."[123] This addition emphasizing the effort of citizens is significant given how many hopes fell flat under the messianic figure of Obama. We cannot wait until we have a clear picture of our final future goals; rather, we must act now in intelligent ways and through inquiry to bring about better conditions and, thereby, truth.[124] And we must be flexible to change and redirect our efforts as they unfold. Meliorism opens up possibilities, collective problem-solving, and the agency necessary for democracy to thrive. For some pragmatists, like Colin Koopman, this meliorism-based hope is "the pragmatist affect par excellence: 'hope is the mood of meliorism,' 'the characteristic attitude of pragmatism is hope.'"[125]

One may not be drawn to a meliorist outlook, though, especially if one's life has been plagued by hardship that makes it difficult to see effort as worthwhile. But such an outlook can be supported with evidence and ultimately fostered. Teachers, religious leaders, and fellow citizens can chart the historical impact of human effort that has demonstrably improved the world. They can reveal goodness and just action even in the midst of or following atrocities of injustice. Meliorism is not Pollyannaish, however, for it acknowledges the lasting blows of moments of despair and the difficulty through which improvement has been won. To showcase the effort and nurture continued hope, people might visit historical locations where significant moments of despair and triumph unfolded, such as the Robben Island Museum in South Africa, where apartheid-era prisoners, such as Nelson Mandela, were held.[126]

While a proclivity to act, pragmatist hope must be cautious and contingent, open to criticism and validation.[127] Because of this, meliorism fits well with democracy as a way of life where our hopes can be nurtured together and where inquiry tests and revises what we believe to be true or desirable. Future-directed meliorism, then, also serves to encourage critique and dissent into problematic ways of being and, through exploring hypotheses about those circumstances, gives rise to action to change them. Additionally, meliorism is aligned with a belief in the agency of people, trusting that they can have significant impact on the world. Their agency is demonstrated not only in the action they undertake to achieve an end-in-view but also in their shaping and revising of the ends-in-view they hold.[128] That said, despite their assertion that people can impact the world, pragmatists must also recognize that there are significant imbalances in who has and can exercise agency and who can influence public policy and practice.[129] Dewey also recognized that action could be inhibited by stagnant and entrenched practices of individuals and culture in a democracy. Certainly, we have witnessed that problem in the cynicism and despair currently growing in America. As a result, Dewey turned to education, arguing that new and more flexible ways of life can be cultivated to fulfill the call to action for improving the world.

Meliorism and Democracy

Meliorism, grounded in inquiry, growth, and truth, unites individuals in social and political hope, as I will detail in the next chapter. Meliorism joins individuals in collective work, which may combat the problems of privatized hope, overreliance on messianic political leaders, cynicism about the future of our society, and tendencies toward authoritarianism discussed in the opening chapter. Koopman says, "As such, meliorism resonates with the central ethical impulse at the heart of pragmatism: democracy. Democracy is the simple idea that political and ethical progress hinges on nothing more than persons, their values, and their actions."[130] This spirit lingers from the founding days of America. And, like Rorty and Green before him, Koopman calls for citizens to work together today, using their radical imaginations, to create a new and better nation and world.

It is meliorism that builds our skills of cultural criticism and sustains the confidence needed to proceed in continually recreating our democratic way of life. Meliorism brings together humanism, which demonstrates that people can impact the world, and pluralism, which shows that there are many different ways of being contingent on many different realities that shape our experience of the world.[131] This spirit has long been demonstrated in American life, yet we find hope struggling today. Reflecting the early roots and corollary growth of pragmatism and democracy, Koopman warns "that a loss of hope is a loss of America itself."[132] As I will flesh out in detail in the next chapter, I intend to show how pragmatist hope draws on our American past to move us forward in the present. It is such hope that can keep America and its democracy vibrant.

3

Hope as Habits

The last chapter began to paint a picture of pragmatist hope by describing its key elements of inquiry, growth, truth, and meliorism. This chapter fleshes out that image by adding in the final important component: habits. Habits are the resources through which we enact hope. Perhaps, for our struggling citizens, habits may be an important part of the answer to their question: "How can I hope?" While one's will can play a significant role in shaping one's outlook on life, one cannot merely choose hope over despair.[133] We require mechanisms that enable us to enact hope and to sustain it across time. And while hope can be a good choice for a citizen to make, it cannot be cast in such easy terms, as something you just personally decide to have or not. Hope does not rely merely on our commitment to it; instead, it is a way of life that grows out of our interactions with others and is facilitated by our habits.

Our unique pattern of habits gives us our distinct characteristics as individuals. But our habits also connect us to other people because our habits are developed alongside and are assessed relative to other people. Notably, habits can be taught and nurtured; they can be revised and improved. This opens opportunities for reviving hope among American adults and for developing hope among children in schools, one of the primary places that we learn habits. In this chapter, I put the final touches on a pragmatist vision of hope. I make a case for the usefulness of such hope, especially for countering and ameliorating some of the struggles we face in America today, but also for the long-term health of our democracy and our future identity as Americans.

Pragmatist Habits

Habits begin with impulses—natural or instinctual urges, often in response to our environment. While the exact makeup and intensity of these impulses vary among people, most of us are born with similar impulses, such as sucking to acquire nutrition and crying when hurt. Dewey explains:

Learning How to Hope. Sarah M. Stitzlein, Oxford University Press (2020). © Oxford University Press.
DOI: 10.1093/oso/9780190062651.001.0001

Man continues to live because ... He is instinct with activities that carry him on. Individuals here and there cave in, and most individuals sag, withdraw and seek refuge at this and that point. But man as man still has the dumb pluck of the animal. He has endurance, hope, curiosity, eagerness, love of action. These traits belong to him by structure, not by taking thought.[134]

These initial sources, aligned with instincts toward survival, are common, but not necessarily present, in all of us. They are largely noncognitive; in other words, we don't stop and think about those behaviors. But those initial inklings do not stay confined to such an individualized and nonreflective location for long. Rather, they quickly make their way into social living and become fodder for reflection and deliberation with others. So, while we may suckle our mother's breast as infants, as we come to understand and reflect on the process of eating, discover tools to assist us, and witness typical ways that our families eat, we move on to eventually use a utensil to deliver solid food to our mouths ourselves.

As we grow and interact with the world around us, we observe and reflect on cultural norms that govern accepted ways of behaving and we begin to craft our impulses into habits. People develop similar habits when they have similar interactions with their environments that tend to reinforce certain patterns of behavior. When those behaviors serve us well by meeting our needs, we tend to do them again and again. When they don't, we reflect on their shortcomings, then tweak or drop those behaviors accordingly. When they function well over time, we increasingly perform those acts without conscious attention until some new situation calls those habits back into consideration. In addition to learning habits from interactions with our environments, we learn them more overtly from people. Their cultivation is most obvious in schools, where we learn about common and socially acceptable behaviors while also imitating the behavior we see from our teachers and peers.

Most people think of habits as dull routines that we repeat exactly— doing the same things in the same ways, though in different places or at different times. But Dewey views habits slightly differently. He sees them as dispositions, proclivities to act in certain ways. Dewey notes, "Any habit marks an *inclination*—an active preference and choice for the conditions involved in its exercise. A habit does not wait, Micawber-like, for a stimulus to turn up so that it may get busy; it actively seeks for occasions to pass into full operation."[135] Habits, then, strive to be put into intelligent action; they are not mere default patterns we thoughtlessly rely on. They are active and energetic; they project themselves.[136] Habits make up our ways of being and we enact them with ease and familiarity because they have proven to help us lead our lives smoothly.

Habits sometimes cause us to desire particular outcomes or objects in order for our lives to flourish. Those desires align with our growth from one experience to the next; they may unite our experiences or serve as ends-in-view to guide us. Importantly, habits also offer a way to pursue those desires, often through thought or bodily movement. For Dewey, habits "do all the perceiving, recognizing, imagining, recalling, judging, conceiving and reasoning that is done."[137] As we encounter new stimuli, habits help us to filter and make sense of those encounters, enabling us to develop ideas about them. They organize our perceptions based on past experiences so that we can form ideas about the world that we test out in order to overcome indeterminate situations. Habits then provide the know-how to act in the world because they entail our working capacities. Finally, we reflect on our experiences and our inquiries to determine which habits bring about our growth by promoting smooth and just transactions with the world and with other people.

Habits take many forms, from the way we carry our bodies (posture, use of personal space) to our tendencies in communicating with others (dominating conversation, listening carefully) to our skills and judgment making (careful consideration, hasty conclusions). Dewey explains, "All habits are demands for certain kinds of activity; and they constitute the self."[138] So, we *are* a collection of habits. Habits shape who and what we are, including how we understand ourselves and how others see us. But, while habits compose us as individuals, they are also intimately linked to other people. They arise from our interactions with others and we reflect on their impact on others as we assess whether they are good ways to continue to act. In other words, we secure our growth and flourishing not merely by pursuing our personal desires, but also by ensuring that we are able to work in coordination with others to achieve mutual well-being. When problematic conditions or novel situations arise, we employ inquiry not just to determine how to change our world, but also to reconsider and reshape our habits so that we can continue to grow and live fruitfully with other people.

It is the intellectual aspect of habits that gives them meaning and keeps people elastic and growing. Good habits are flexible, enabling us to respond to our changing world and carrying us over from one experience to the next, thereby bringing about growth. Bad habits, however, are those that become fixed and disconnected from intelligence. Much like the problems of latching on to unchanging goals described in the last chapter, bad habits are restrictive and have a hold on us, rather than us on them. Bad habits freeze plasticity, disabling the conditions for growth.[139] Dewey explains: "the acquiring of habits is due to an original plasticity of our natures: to our ability to vary responses till we find an appropriate and efficient way of acting. Routine habits, and habits that possess us instead of our possessing them, are habits which put an end to plasticity. They mark the close of power to vary."[140] When we are deep in despair, our selves may come apart. Unsure of how to proceed, our habits may flounder. We may then succumb to bad habits that lack flexibility. In our political lives, these might include cynicism or apathy, which render our lives stagnant and fail to keep up with the changing world. But rather than reconciling ourselves to such a state, Dewey's philosophy offers us ways of life that can help to reorient us.

In the context of democracy, a bad habit is one that keeps democracy from functioning well. It may be one that is stagnant and doesn't keep up with the changing population or social needs, is exclusionary, blocks interactions with others, or is unjust. Essentially, a bad habit is one that keeps us from adapting in the ways we need to as we encounter new situations involving our fellow citizens or our shared experiences. In my first book, I detailed bad habits of race and racism.[141] American democracy has long been plagued by habits of privileging white people over others. These habits, for example, impact the way we hear, fail to hear, or ignore the perspectives and experiences of people of color, thereby shaping a democracy where not all participants are fully equal and where the interests of some citizens are weighted more heavily than others as we determine common goods and just desserts for individuals.

We cannot easily drop bad habits, but we can work through a process of changing and replacing them with better habits that are more just or inclusive. Ideally, because habits are "adjustments of the environment, not merely to it," adopting new habits (through a careful process of intellectual reflection or education) can change the environmental phenomena that produced the problematic old habit, in this case possibly making democracy better or reducing racism.[142] For example, a white child raised in an all-white family and neighborhood may develop a bad habit of only interacting with other white children at his integrated school. The child may choose to self-segregate when selecting peers to sit with at school, thereby engaging in an exclusionary practice that prevents him from learning from children of color or learning how to work across differences. A novel situation may arise, such as joining a county-wide baseball team largely populated by children of color, leaving the child unsure of how to play with his new teammates as a result of this lack of cross-racial interaction. Reflecting on this situation and discussing the struggle with his teacher might prompt a change to his seating habit at school. Selecting a new seat with children of color not only changes his opportunities for new interactions and growth but also changes the environment, presenting new opportunities for other classmates.[143]

There is a reciprocal relationship between habits and thought. Habits enable us to test our ideas and then reflect on those experiments to see whether the idea is worthwhile and whether we need to adjust our habits or develop new ones. Similarly, when we find ourselves in an indeterminate situation, we consider our habits. When we learn to form habits tentatively, as hypotheses about how we might best act in unpredictable future circumstances, habits can become flexible agents of change whose form emerges as situations unfold. Or, in Dewey's words, "the intellectual element in a habit fixes the relation of the habit to varied and elastic use, and hence to continued growth."[144] When habits are tied to intelligent reflection and inquiry, they are projective and sites of agency.

Understanding Hope as Habits

We arrive now at my chief contribution to understanding hope and the foundation for how we might cultivate a form of hope capable of reviving democracy in America. I contend that *hope, as a set of habits and their enactment, is most essentially a disposition toward possibility and change for the betterment of oneself and, typically, others*. It is a way of being that overcomes the paralysis of pessimism by bringing together proclivities and intelligent reflection to motivate one to act while providing a sustainable structure for doing so. Hope is a way of projecting ourselves toward a better future, positioning us toward action. In Dewey's words, pragmatist habits of hope are "active attitudes of welcome."[145] They are ways we greet the world and are disposed toward action in it.

Unlike common understanding of habits as mere thoughtless, repeated action, pragmatist habits of hope are attitudes and dispositions that shape how we transact with the world. They often lead us to seek out or create possibilities when we face challenges. Differing from individualist accounts of hope in terms of desire for a self-serving goal or faith in other savior figures, habits of hope entail action that moves us toward better ways of living. Hope helps us envision a desired future that arises practically out of our conditions and with knowledge of the past. Yet, we move beyond those conditions through assessing possibilities, determining whether outcomes are desirable, and imagining how we might rearrange our circumstances to achieve new and better conditions.[146] For Dewey, imagination heads off failures that can derail hope because "thought runs ahead and foresees outcomes."[147]

Unlike other accounts that put hope in a savior figure or in a distant and unchanging goal, pragmatist habits of hope respond to the problems of the present using knowledge of the past so that we can craft a better future ourselves. These habits support us as we test hypotheses and imagine ways that we might reconstruct our circumstances in order to better our lives.

Hope theorist Alan Mittleman argues that hope is not just about change, however. He rightly argues that hope can also be about maintaining conditions that help us flourish. I would add that even when intended to preserve, hope is about change away from how things are currently going or the direction in which they are trending, where those long-standing conditions we value may be in jeopardy.

The practical, intelligent, and generative nature of pragmatist hope leads contemporary pragmatist Patrick Shade to rightly conclude that it entails "conditioned transcendence," where hope has two modes: "being grounded in real conditions and being productive of new and better ones."[148] Pragmatist hope focuses on the agency of people in realistic settings, rather than resorting to supernatural forces or optimistic pipe dreams. But it also recognizes that hope must be realistic and generative, otherwise, as in the case of the poor and racial minority citizens urged to keep on hoping in spite of a long history of seeming insurmountable injustices, "If hoping exhausts our resources, it is better not to hope."[149]

Pragmatist hope also emphasizes intelligence, where "Intelligence is critical method applied to goods of belief, appreciation and conduct, so as to construct freer and more secure goods. . . . [I]t is the reasonable object of our deepest faith and loyalty, the stay and support of all reasonable hopes."[150] Michael Eldridge adds an important point, linking intelligence and democracy:

Intelligence as criticism is the transformation of what is in terms of what might be preferable. Democracy in the wide sense is the public transformation of experience, the constructing of "freer and more secure goods" by mean of the "free communication of shareable meanings." This deliberative, communicative, constructive process, when considered from a social psychological (or less well-defined) perspective is intelligence, but when considered from a political perspective is democracy.[151]

Here we see the weaving together of a Deweyan account of inquiry and growth with the social and political practices of shared living.

Many citizens today tend to proclaim whether they do or do not "have hope," as though hope is an object that is passively possessed. Pragmatist habits of hope, however, are better understood as a verb—hoping, an on-going activity we do, often, with or alongside others. As we hope, we use our imagination to construct creative solutions and envision using our agency to impact the world and change our circumstances. Most people overestimate how much control they have over the future; yet when we choose to act, we need courage because we always face unpredictability, no matter how well we plan and how much control we have.[152] Courage considers and assesses risks, uses intelligence and resourcefulness to determine means to desired ends and to recognize the limits of our control, and then willingly faces those risks in order to pursue that end. Imagination, resourcefulness, courage, and agency operate hand-in-hand as elements of hoping.

Such emphasis on agency and action suggests that we should not stand idly by, as we see many citizens doing today in the face of significant social problems. Nor should we throw up our hands in the air, asserting that we've lost some object called 'hope,' for hope is within us and is realized in our actions. It is not something we hold or claim, but rather something we are in the practice of doing or can flexibly develop when needed. It may not be *in* our hands, but it's *on* our shoulders. We should not be left to our own devices, however, or bear weighty culpability when we fall short or find ourselves exhausted by our best efforts. For hope, as I will argue in the next chapter, suggests collective work to ameliorate knotty social issues. Hoping is not up to us alone.

Habits of hope, as well as the process of inquiry and problem-solving, can be intentionally cultivated. This suggests heightened need and opportunity for schools to nurture hope in students and to help them enact it well, which I will address in detail in the final chapter. For now, let me say that schools can help burgeoning citizens to assess which habits are fruitful, so they can learn tools to continually keep themselves aligned with and engaged in hoping.

Interaction with people who demonstrate and act on hope can foster agency and courage in others and motivate them to take hopeful action themselves. Relatedly, "Our sense of possibility may depend on our seeing that others are acting on behalf of similar goals."[153] Schools, located in communities that may share similar goals, are ripe spaces for demonstrating such action and spreading hope.

The Social and Political Elements of Pragmatist Hope

A pragmatist account of hope, which arises out of inquiry, truth, growth, meliorism, and habits, bridges together the individual with the social and political. Hope connects us to other people and situates us within a network of power, where groups influence one another as they pursue their desired good life. In this section, I'll discuss how that works and why it is a useful understanding and practice of hope to apply in today's context. To set the stage, Dewey says in *Creative Democracy*, "democracy is a personal way of individual life. . . . Instead of thinking of our own dispositions and habits as accommodated to certain institutions, we have to learn to think of the latter as expressions, projections and extensions of habitually dominant personal attitudes."[154] Notice how Dewey flips the typical understanding; instead of democracy shaping who we are, we may shape democracy. How radical to rethink of democracy as a projection of our own hoping.

To begin, hope is more than just an aspect of our inner lives, our pursuit of self-serving goals, or our faith in a deity. Rather, hope emerges amid specific contexts, thereby raising implications for shared social living. While habits of hope are located within and compose individuals, hope is not individualist. Habits grow out of our individual impulses, but those impulses are later shaped by our community, often taking the form of customs. Habits of hope employ the resources of our community and relationships to provide means for us to pursue our ends-in-view. And many of those ends-in-view have been influenced by those around us, as we talk with them about our desires, witness popular desires of others, and more. Pragmatist hope extends into the social world and is fruitful there because it is guided by growth and meliorism, each of which takes into consideration the well-being of others. It pushes us from individual pursuit of our goals to reflective, collective public work to make the physical, social, and political world a better place.

For Dewey, problem-solving is seldom done alone; rather, we must reach out to others to collect their interpretations of the current state of affairs and suggestions for change. Anthropologist Lia Haro, who studied and quotes the Zapatistas, an entire culture based on hope, concluded: "Hope is tended and increased in dialogue and receptive listening: 'Our hope grows and we become better because we know how to listen.' The political dimension of insurgent hope, of creating a different future, requires the work of listening and speaking with others to find 'pockets of light' and possibility that would be invisible without the advantage of multiple, distinct perspectives."[155] She rightfully draws attention to the fact that hoping requires listening in order to discover and pursue new possibilities, especially when they have the potential to impact the lives of others. In Dewey's words, we need "an attitude of mind which actively welcomes suggestions and relevant information from all sides."[156]

Hoping engages in open-minded listening and collaboration; it brings people together rather than distances them, as cynicism does. While listening often is confined to only our most immediate relationships or communities, the increasing interconnectedness of our decisions and implications on others should urge us to listen to and include others—something pragmatist Judith Green dubs "a global network of social hope."[157] Hoping connects us to other people, some of whom may also be engaged in hoping. Listening to others who may be impacted by our aims or who may hold conflicting goals may reveal imbalances of power or injustice at play. Pausing the march toward action and opening ourselves to truly listen to the views and competing accounts of others, including seeking out the perspectives of minority communities, can help us craft not only more feasible visions but also more just ones. Inquiry and meliorism connect us to an understanding of the past and visions of the future, including those held by others. These connections between people, ideas, and imaginative visions provide us with resources needed to pursue our ends-in-view and enable us to see that we can, indeed, improve the world.

Let me pause here to consider President Trump's call to "Make America Great Again (MAGA)," which echoed similar slogans used earlier by Ronald Reagan, George H. W. Bush, and Bill Clinton. This slogan certainly invokes a sense of improving our lives and our country, though perhaps not as strongly as the alternatives he first considered, including "We Will Make America Great" and "Make America Great."[158] But many Trump supporters picked it up in a way that fell victim to some of the problems of privatized hope I described earlier. It could have been a forward-driven call to remember the best of our past, to draw on those successes as evidence of Americans' power to rebuild anew, and then to use that past to shape a better direction for the future. But rather than asking, "Great for whom?," many Trump supporters stopped at individually reflecting on previous times that were better for them or their families. They did not engage in listening to the accounts of others who did not fare well during those times (for a host of reasons, including racism and sexism that were prominent during the popular period of the 1950s that many supporters nostalgically recalled).[159] They did not engage in open-minded listening to or collaboration with those different from themselves—skills important to successful work in today's political context where we tend to seek out like-minded perspectives of those politically and demographically similar to us. Instead, the hats bearing the slogan became not just a marker of support for Trump, but a way for citizens to identify peers yearning for the return of better days, assuming that their visions were shared even when not discussed.[160] As a result, the hope conveyed in MAGA was not checked by inquiry or experience, nor confirmed for its role in bringing about a flourishing life, leaving it uninformed and largely unsustainable. It also precluded discussions about what the ends-in-view of MAGA were and what actions citizens might take to achieve them, leading some citizens to turn over the task to the president, as evidenced in the inauguration day interviews I noted in chapter 1.

Hoping moves us beyond ourselves, connecting us not only to other people but also to "what was" and the "not yet."[161] Through such connections we find resources to pursue our ends-in-view and develop a sense of accomplishment—an assurance that in cooperation with others, we can envision and craft a better world without relying merely on the promises of politicians or throwing up our hands in isolated resignation. Akiba Lerner powerfully urges that we must "embrace the radical contingency that our personal hopes are connected to our ability to mutually recognize, create dialogue with, and help actualize the hopes of our fellow citizens."[162] Such contingency and mutual dependence, alongside agency and action, serve as important counters to trends we see among citizens today.

Hope and Trust

Pragmatist hope relies on trust—trust in each other and trust in the ability of people to positively impact the world. And, importantly, engaging in hope also builds trust. There are many reasons why trust is struggling in America today: from increased polarization to corruption and scandals that render us leery of elected officials to a context of neoliberal competition that champions each of us enterprising for our own personal success and leaves us suspicious of anyone else who might get in our way. In response, pragmatist hope demonstrates, at best, a spirit of togetherness and a "we" of political life, and, at minimum, an acknowledgment of our necessary relationships with others and the idea that achieving our own well-being is often dependent on fruitful interactions with them.

In other words, as hope urges us to act to improve our lives, we may discover shortcomings in our abilities or come to see that our efforts are enhanced or more successful when paired with others. Conceding the limitations of our own agency, we are ushered into trusting others. They may pick up where we leave off, fill in the gaps where we fall short, or they may empower and expand our own agency. But we must also be leery of naive trust, where we may jeopardize our well-being or that of others by trusting people who seek to take advantage of us. When we recognize our limitations in fulfilling our particular hopes, we expose our vulnerability by turning to others for help or support in achieving our aims. Sometimes, through dialogue about shared needs, our particular aims become shared aims or are revised due to mutual consideration.

This is done, in part, through careful consideration of those who have acted harmfully or maliciously in the past and guarded willingness to work with them again, often under conditions where previous harms are named and attended to. It is also done through open communication about motives, consequences, risks, and benefits. Such restorative and open discussion is especially important within the context of racism, where many minority citizens are rightfully leery of some of their white peers, especially within the context of white supremacy, which may embolden some white people to take advantage of citizens of color.

Trust and support don't just move in one direction. Hopers should engage in mutually supportive activities together. Victoria McGeer explains,

> Hoping well thus involves cultivating a meta-disposition in which some of one's hopeful energy becomes directed toward supporting the hopeful agency of others and, hence, toward creating the kind of environment in which one's own hopeful energy is supplemented by the hopeful energy renewed in them. In this way, hoping well draws less on

the egocentric preoccupations of desire and of dread and more on the alterocentric concerns of care.[163]

When we project an image of that peer as trustworthy and capable to them, we lend the energy of our hope to scaffold them in enacting their agency.[164] As a result, "when we hope in each other, reciprocally, we make a commitment to each other in addition to that made to our shared objective of hope."[165] It is the forming of this "we," this mutual care through hoping together that can help reaffirm the value of democracy and shared political life. Such a caring community can support the hoping of its members, nurturing their agency, while also creating an environment that fosters communally endorsed and pursued ends.

We know that democracies work better when they are small, enabling citizens to know each other, to feel committed to each other, and thereby trust one another. But within the American context of 325 million citizens, those committed and trusting communities are often only confined to our families, neighborhoods, or local Civil organizations. Yet, it has been well documented that when we work on local issues with or in close proximity to someone significantly different from ourselves, we become more trustful of not only that person but also others who share his demographic characteristics. This suggests the possibility of opening up networks of burgeoning trust by starting with small or local projects.

In order for trust to work on a national scale, I follow Charles Taylor in calling for a "strong collective identity" where we have a commitment to doing common work together.[166] I contend that part of that work is engaging in hoping together. In a rather cyclical way, we may form a shared identity when we hope together. We may extend the feelings of mutual concern and trust that we are more likely to hold in our immediate contexts or develop while working on local projects into larger practices of democratic living in a spirit of shared fate so that we may develop a collective identity around democracy and hope. Such a large community may also bolster our feelings of belonging and security, thereby addressing some citizens who feel "left behind," those who feel distrust in members of opposing political parties, and those who may fear that others will render them or the country unsafe.

Unlike positive psychology, which uses a Snyder scale to measure hope without considering its impact on others, and unlike individualist accounts that are self-serving, pragmatist hope is social and political. It is guided by the need to work with and flourish alongside other citizens who are all deeply embedded in long-standing battles over power and recognition. Whereas contemporary American democracy is plagued by apathy about social problems, distrust of the motives of others, white supremacy, and civic disengagement, pragmatist hope pushes us into the fray of those problems, urging trust in others and action alongside them. Pragmatist hope shifts one's identity from self-serving individual to belonging to a collective "we" of hopers. Such an identity enables citizens to better detect social problems and recognize their mutual stake in them, rather than passively or cynically sitting by.[167] I'm not saying that we can make a sudden switch from being disengaged and distrustful individuals, but when cultivating pragmatist habits of hope is integrated across civil life and schooling, we can slowly make such an important transition and can sustain that effort through larger democratic habits that I describe in chapter 6.

We have a tendency to think of our constitutional republic democracy in terms of its formalist components, like having a constitution and enabling citizens to vote for leaders to represent them. But for Dewey and other pragmatists, a focus on habits shows that democracy is also cultural. It is a way of living—patterns of behavior, inclinations, and proclivities aligned with shared social living, addressing communal problems, and developing organizations of people and environments that support the flourishing of citizens. To revive democracy is not merely to reassert the institutions and laws of government, but rather to breathe new life into cultural practices of togetherness, trust, and mutual concern. Habits of hope are integral to such an improved democratic future, as I will explain in the next chapter.

Benefits of Pragmatist Hope

Throughout my description of pragmatist habits of hope, I've highlighted some of its strengths as a philosophical account and its usefulness in American life today. In this section I want to summarize its benefits as a whole in order to justify why citizens not only should cultivate hope but also should embrace pragmatist hope rather than some other approach.

Notably, pragmatist hope heads off some potentially problematic outcomes or forms of hope, such as the self-centered obsessions that we may develop, like the aforementioned marathon training. It is also possible, under other forms of hope, to hope for something that is harmful to others because it may benefit the particular hoper. While there may be some legitimacy to reasons for desiring harmful aims and they may provoke initial hope, actually engaging in the pragmatist process of inquiry would likely deter or end action to achieve them. Remember that pragmatist habits of hope are a disposition toward possibility and change for the betterment of oneself and, typically, others. Through inquiry and experimentation, we determine what ways of life allow ourselves and others to flourish. We may not know the outcomes of our hoping when we start our projects, but pragmatist hope entails the sort of ongoing checks and reflections that would cause us to stop when our project proves harmful or the consequences don't lead us to growth or out of ruts.

Pragmatist hope, then, contains a process that helps to keep our hopes aligned with things and activities that enable ourselves and others to live fruitful lives. Within the pragmatist process of inquiry, proponents need to do their due diligence in reaching out to wider communities to gather their perspectives and perhaps even include them with a spirit of solidarity to ensure that their hope is wise and justified. Admittedly, this can be a challenging standard. There may be times when it is unfair or inappropriate to ask oppressed groups, in particular, to bear the effort of continued reaching out and listening, such as black citizens who have born considerable harms by engaging with racists and may need to protect themselves or find ways to cope that cut off continued interactions. The expectation of listening to opposing peers can similarly stymie groups championing identity groups who may intentionally exclude competing views or members of other demographic groups in order to protect themselves from harm, prevent the foreclosure of new ideas by naysayers, and more.

Perhaps pragmatism's staying power and its relative resurgence recently stems from its being firmly grounded in real-life struggles, while striving to improve everyday life. Such an orientation is ripe for supporting a realistic yet robust concept of hope that appeals to Americans. First, a pragmatist concept of hope weds thought and action, yielding hope that is a practical and wisely driven activity, as opposed to positing hope as a fixed trait or desire that is possessed and wielded. It derives its directions from imagination as well as pluralistic and inclusive inquiry with others. Relatedly, a pragmatist conception of hope that is located within the complex circumstances of everyday life, rather than simply being applied regardless of circumstances, as is the case in the sense of hope often attributed to children and popular in contemporary theories of grit in schools, which I will explain in the next chapter. Finally, pragmatist hope is connected to life's activities, and hope can direct these activities as outcomes of habits and imagination. It is not a sense of entitlement as one anticipates a specific future, which can lead one to passively wait, and then to be angry when it doesn't arrive.[168] It's a bent toward action and a willingness to take risks as one's complicated path unfolds.

The shared work of democracy that rises from pragmatist hope is more fruitful and just than mere independent wishes, optimism, or grit because the well-being of others plays a key role in constructing narratives of the future and determining whether or not our ideas are true and our ways of living promote growth. This pragmatist version of hope is tied to the growth of individuals and the well-being of communities. It has the ability to bring together individuals into democratic communities, unlike other accounts of hope that focus on an individual's feelings or a god figure. The active sense of hoping urges us to take some level of responsibility for shaping our lives, in part by hoping with others. Rather than throwing in the towel when facing difficult problems, it's a call to do something about them and a practice that can build our agency and that of others.

Insofar as it can be cultivated as a set of habits, we have the ability to nurture pragmatist hope and stave off the debilitating impact of apathy, cynicism, pessimism, and loss of faith in democratic living. This ability reveals that one's hope is not fixed, but rather may be targeted and educated. Both the content of one's hopes and the practice of hoping may be cultivated. Such a view opens up considerable avenues for reviving hope in America today. In sum, a pragmatist theory of hope is realistic, flexible, social, generative, and educable.

Shortcomings of Pragmatist Hope

While there is much to celebrate about pragmatist hope, it also presents some potential shortcomings. First, those who've held a relatively privileged position in society or in life in general may be more inclined to support this view, which may appear utopian or naive to those who've faced significant hardship. What I mean here is that pragmatist habits of hope may seem reasonable to people, like myself, who have generally led lives where things have gone well and have not had to face significant, prolonged despair or personal struggle. That's not to say that I and others don't feel significantly troubled over the suffering of other people; indeed, we may feel outraged or forlorn in response to the plight of others. Nor is it to say that I and others hold an optimistic view, assuming that things will necessarily work out for the best for ourselves. Instead, we simply have not personally encountered overwhelming, intense, and long-term despair to really test whether our enactment of hope can withstand such strains. Nor, as a white woman, have I had to face, for example, structural racism, which can exhaust even ardent hopers. In other words, is this account of hope muscular and robust enough to really do the heavy lifting needed in the face of great problems?

In order to take potential objections seriously and provide a few responses, let me briefly consider one example that is representative of the sort that may press against or challenge my account of hope: sustaining the hope of African Americans in the face of entrenched and systemic racism, despite continued attempts to end the problem. Yes, pragmatist hope, with its varying efforts across time and environments, may give people of color some temporary or partial respite from the strain of racism, even if that only happens in moments where they are merely imagining a better and more just world, rather than actually getting to live in one. I'm reminded here of gospel songs and stories, which have played a significant role in tiding over those in the midst of struggle. Stories of a land of justice and plenty may provide some level of comfort when enduring the opposite, especially when considering what the future might bring. Surely, they have played a significant role in the courageous lives and efforts of exceptional champions of racial justice like Ida B. Wells and Sojourner Truth. But, they are likely not sufficient to sustain the sort of ongoing, challenging work that pragmatist hoping poses of ordinary individuals and groups of people who require clear-eyed hoping from day to day. And if such stories put too much emphasis on the role of the Savior, they can risk becoming an opiate that pacifies one during hardship, rather than provoking action or even justified outrage.

Prominent pragmatist and African American thinker Cornel West has responded to the situation of structural racism and white supremacy with hope. To begin, he provides a unique contribution to pragmatist hope by tracing the roots of his musically inspired "blues" version of hope to the struggles of black folks in America. He attends carefully to the harms of the past as he considers hopeful visions of the future. He contends that despair and hope are often intimately connected. He explains, "It is impossible to look honestly at our catastrophic conditions and not have some despair—it is a healthy sign of how deeply we care. It is also a mark of maturity—a rejection of cheap American optimism."[169] Rather than a mere rose-colored glasses outlook on life, West recognizes that things are, in many ways, not getting better, and he points to the history of his race for evidence. And he extends care to his black peers by acknowledging the seriousness of their plight, even as he calls for continued effort in the face of it.

But importantly, his call to meliorism is one that upholds a belief that other people—namely whites—can do better. As such, it entails a historically informed and wary trust in others. He says, "I never give up on any human being no matter what color, because I believe they all have potential."[170] Moreover, his meliorism is driven by virtues that enable one to flourish as one faces despair, a drive "to try to keep struggling for more love, more justice, more freedom, and more democracy."[171] Such a hope—one that is closely connected to a painful history and ongoing suffering—is, as he says, "always blood-stained and tear-soaked." [172] Whereas his pragmatist predecessors established that hope must always attend to and grow out of the real conditions of our lives, West drives home the point that those conditions are often quite horrid, and that hope is closely related to the despair that those conditions cause. But his call to effort in spite of and because of those conditions is strong: "Real hope is grounded in a particularly messy struggle and it can be betrayed by naïve projections of a better future that ignore the necessity of doing the real work. So what we are talking about is *hope on a tightrope*."[173] West recognizes the difficult and precarious position of hoping.

West's version of hope is situated within his account of prophetic pragmatism. Though I will not detail prophetic pragmatism here, it is worthwhile to point out that it entails the sort of critical outlook that I will say more about in the next chapter. It arises from an informed understanding of the atrocities of the past as well as frustrations revealed when our world falls short of visions of what could be—understandings shaped by the accounts of prose and poetry. Such a "critical temper," as West calls it, takes despair head on with an "experimental disposition" and a faith in the ability of people to work democratically together.[174] "The critical temper motivated by democratic faith yields all-embracing moral and/or religious visions that project credible ameliorative possibilities grounded in present realities in light of systemic structural analyses of the causes of social misery (without reducing all misery to historical causes)."[175] As a result, West calls for hope as a sort of cultural criticism that reveals injustice, pushes us to act on that injustice, and sustains us through our experiments to alleviate such injustice. For West, this prophetic, blues hope is bolstered by habits of courage and Christian love, which is focused less on a savior figure and more on how people can support each other.[176]

Black public intellectual Ta-Nehisi Coates, whom some have deemed an Afro-pessimist or black atheist, provides a counterview to West, asserting that hope can be harmful. He closes his letter to his son about racism by also issuing a call.[177] He urges his son to struggle on behalf of himself and his ancestors who've sought freedom and safety for their black bodies. And he urges his son to struggle not under the false pretense that his son's struggle will convert racists to the ways of justice, but rather to recognize that racists and white people who benefit from racism must also "learn to struggle themselves."[178] Coates warns that our "goal-oriented" era poses too many magical and quick fixes for the problems of white supremacy, and chooses instead to focus on the spaces of refuge, pleasure, and comfort that black people have created for themselves within the midst of oppression.[179] Eddie Glaude also highlights "Black churches, social clubs, schools and colleges, newspapers, masonic orders, and fraternal and sororal organizations."[180] He explains that those "institutions afforded African Americans spaces to deliberate, to think, to organize—to breathe. They are (or were) key sites for black democratic life, especially in a country where black lives aren't as valued as other people's lives. They provided the elbow room to challenge white supremacy."[181] So while Coates emphasizes these spaces as providing some escape from despair related to white supremacy, Glaude seems to endorse using them for refuge as one practices democratically living among safe peers, and as one reenergizes and plans for continued effort to end racism while engaged with whites.

While his call to struggle may seem aligned with meliorism, Coates does not endorse collective political action as a way to wipe out racism. He argues that those who call for such transformation are naive, warns that those who write with a hopeful spirit tend toward presenting only myths about the triumphs of justice rather than facts about its shortcomings, and asserts that he does not have hope that America will significantly change to end racism.[182] He sees racial progress, if even possible, as always connected to deep injustice, and when he tries to imagine a better world taking shape, he fears the violence and injustice that might accompany it.[183] As a result, he endorses a form of political fatalism, largely accepting racism as a native and enduring way of life in America.

Pragmatist Melvin Rogers, aligned with my spirit of meliorism, summarizes and counters: "But there is a sleight of hand in Coates's 'black atheism'; it conflates hope with certainty, and hope becomes our fatal flaw. Yet we don't need to believe that progress is inevitable to think that, through our efforts, we may be able to move toward a more just society. We can, however, be sure that no good will come of the refusal to engage in this work."[184] By conflating hope with certainty, Coates confused hope with optimism—the belief that things will necessarily work out for the best. And the appropriate opposite of optimism is pessimism. By retreating to pessimism, he similarly upholds a certainty that things will not improve, as Rogers calls out. Coates, then, has not so much debunked hope, as optimism. Moreover, my account of hope is more nuanced than some critiques might expect. Rogers, a meliorist, holds open possibility for improvement and wisely showcases how Black Lives Matter has produced impact through transforming voices who have experienced injustice into action for justice by working locally to identify problems and craft and implement solutions.

Taking a different stand on struggle and outlook on the future of race in America, I'm reminded of Langston Hughes's description of incredible suffering and simultaneous hope that America can improve and one day may fulfill what he seemed to see as its ideals. As a result, he pledges his allegiance to America as a place of adapting justice earned through hard work and struggle in his poem, "Let America be America Again"—a harkening to the experimental spirit of America and its quest to be freer and more equitable. Unlike Coates, who sees America as a rather finished tale, Hughes believed that there is still much of the story to write.

Glaude urges that in the writing of the story of American democracy we must first recognize that the paradigm of American ideas has long been bound up with practices of white supremacy. We cannot simply achieve a better life by working harder to ensure the principles of democracy if we fail to see how deeply entangled they have been with race and class privilege. We must overtly describe the devastating impact of valuing some people more than others as we craft a new, more expansive notion of democracy. Writing a new story of democracy can also change our identity within it. "We can create new identities together that take traumatic pasts into account, rather than turning our past into celebrations of progress."[185]

Martin Luther King Jr. sought to transform the "fatigue of despair into the buoyancy of hope."[186] And he even tried to best his racist opponents with the claim, "be assured that we will wear you down by our capacity to suffer."[187] But there is hard evidence illustrating that racism takes a sizable toll on people of color. Even King was hospital-bound, feeling down, and battling exhaustion on the very day he found out he won the Nobel Prize for his efforts.[188] In a racist culture, many bodies of color are breaking down, increasingly susceptible to illness, and continually exhausted. Philosophers Calvin Warren and pragmatist Shannon Sullivan warn about these physical ramifications.[189] Sullivan, in the pragmatist spirit of assessing truth by looking at the impact of the effects of racism on health, adds that African Americans would do better to stop hoping for an end to racism. Instead, they should start working on new habits and coping mechanisms that enable them to flourish within the racist world and set their sights on other, more useful and feasible goals for ensuring fruitful lives.

Like Coates, Warren and Sullivan also address the problem of constantly telling minority people to pursue what increasingly looks to be an impossible goal: the defeat of racism. In some regards, this seems to be a form of cruel optimism, always directed to the future and always out of reach, asserting with certainty a progress that doesn't pan out. In other regards, "political hope," as Warren dubs it, holds that political action is the only legitimate avenue for pursuing the end of racism, while other forms of resistance, coping, or struggle (such as those championed by Coates and described by Glaude) are seen as not doing anything at all. As a result, Warren claims, "we must hope for the end of political hope."[190] I recognize that my case for adopting habits of hope is not drastically different from being pressured to pursue political hope via political activism, though I intend for my practices of hoping to be wider and more flexible, providing for an array of resistance, coping, and imaginative strategies. But like the theorists of political hope via activism, and the theorists of grit I describe in chapter 5, the risk is conveying to people of color that they must conform to some dominant-dictated mold of behavior in order to earn a better and happier life. I intend, however, for my account to be more open, more nuanced, and more inviting.

These criticisms do reveal some worrisome implications of pragmatist hoping and suggest shortcomings with my approach and that of West. At the very least, the call to ongoing effort to alleviate racism may invite continued suffering when effort might well be better spent elsewhere to forge spaces and means of protection from harm. And, pragmatist hope may not be strong enough to endure ongoing effort unless there is more motivation for the whites benefiting from privilege to step up to share the load, while at the same time knocking down the hierarchies that support them. What the example of racial suffering and the wide variety of political experiences in America does expose is that there may be particular moments or situations where people are justified in not embracing or enacting the form of political hope I describe in this book. This does not mean that pragmatist political hope falls short of the general needs for political life, civic engagement, or citizenship education I emphasize in these pages. This matter of racism and turning away from hope is certainly not closed and is worthy of much more attention, but addressing it in more detail is beyond the primary focus and space permitted here.

Other criticisms of pragmatist hope rise from the reliance on individuals upholding meliorism. Evidence from the Gallup World Poll shows that "the vast majority of people on the planet think their lives will be better in time . . . generally believing that tomorrow holds some promise, and that things can change for the better."[191] Yet, continual encounters with terrible situations that reveal appalling elements of human conduct may lead one to doubt the possibility of humans positively improving the world in substantial ways. While I claimed earlier that preachers, teachers, and community leaders can teach about the history of success in one's community, the personal experiences of some individuals may run counter to the evidence for meliorism presented and the collective body of evidence for ongoing harm or injustice may outweigh signs of improvement or justice. Personally confronting atrocious human acts may rightfully make one suspect of evidence for meliorism.

Or, individuals who lack significant power, social positioning, money, or other elements that influence their ability to impact the world, may doubt their own agency and therefore avoid making effort, seeing it as impossible or a waste of time. Relatedly, truly dire situations where human effort is extremely limited (those dying of terminal diseases, those constrained in concentration campus during the Holocaust) may decrease the meaningfulness and usefulness of pragmatist hope. In some of those situations, especially those that are more personal and less tied to social or political life, a more religious notion of hope may be a better approach to help people transcend those conditions, even if only in spirit. In light of this, I want to be clear that, to engage in pragmatist hope, people often need to first have their basic needs met. Those needs include not only fundamentals like food and shelter but also a sufficient degree of self-determination and influence over decisions that affects one's life. Asking those whose needs are unmet to take up and sustain pragmatist hoping may simply be too great of a burden, though they certainly can develop habits of hope and extend some effort. Instead, this prerequisite reveals that those whose needs have been generally met have a greater responsibility to hope and to take action in service of change.[192]

Finally, pragmatist hope is a largely collective endeavor. Yet, our current environment increasingly lacks a sense of a "we" that works together.

Many citizens are increasingly hostile toward public projects and even public things (schools, parks), which are often a part of the sort of hoping and its ends-in-view that I describe. This environment poses considerable obstacles for practicing pragmatist hope, even if doing so may actually nurture such a "we." This is, in part, why I, like Dewey before me, turn to beginning early with children, thinking that within schools we may be able to reach them before debilitating worldviews fully take hold. Yet, I also recognize that I may be asking too much of schools that are already strapped with teaching content, sustaining communities, and more. Not to mention that schools have a tendency to reproduce the status quo rather than change it, as hoping might urge.

The situation for older students in colleges and universities also faces challenges, though of a different sort. Institutions of higher education have long been communities of inquiry that tackle vexing social and scientific problems. Yet, recently some citizens have become less trustful of those institutions, especially when dealing with politically controversial issues. Some question the usefulness of such inquiry and desire a focus on learning more narrow job skills that serve the individual and economy instead.[193] Relatedly, some citizens are skeptical of science as a whole, a discipline and approach central to pragmatist inquiry and university-based research, and more so of science being conducted in controversial areas like vaccination, climate change, and genetically modified food.[194]

Acknowledging these shortcomings, I turn in the next chapter to articulating the connection between hope and democracy. Democracy is a relationship where we test out hoping together, continually revising and reconstructing our environments to meet our mutual ends-in-view and to sustain human flourishing. We hope with others, rather than merely by ourselves. The democratic community becomes a concrete location and source for both forming the objects of our hope and engaging in hoping—an important place where we can sort out "What should I hope for?" and "How can I hope?"

4

Hope and Democracy

Now that we have a working definition of what hope is, I want to explain why it matters for democracy, before turning to how we might learn how to hope to round out the book. Facing despair and a struggling democracy, many Americans are asking, "How can I hope?" and "What should I hope for?" Focusing on the relationship between hope and democracy, which I articulate in this chapter, offers not only an enriched understanding of *how* we hope together but also particular content of *what* we might hope for within our country. And it offers insight into how democracy and hope are mutually supportive of one another. Given the current struggles faced by our citizens and our democracy, this relationship suggests that valuing and nurturing hope may be one important way to sustain and strengthen our democracy today and, especially, over time and into the future.

Recall that hope functions as a verb—the active process of hoping—but hope also may have particular objects or objectives that serve as ends-in-view. The objects are things (sometimes public things like parks and clean water)[195] we desire and the objectives are events or states of affairs that we want to bring to fruition (such as enjoyable employment that brings financial stability).[196] Those objects and objectives may help us make our way out of indeterminate situations, satisfying our needs or resolving our problems so that we can grow and move forward.[197] While these examples might sound quite large or ambitious, objects and objectives as ends-in-view are often smaller aims that may string together with others across time toward larger outcomes. For example, my husband and I might first reflect on our frustrating experience of detachment from others and consider ways to create opportunities to get to know and interact with families in our community. Then we might gather with a neighbor to discuss our desire to get to know others in our area better and brainstorm potential ways to do so. Next, we might set up a designated play space for children on our street to see if other families are looking for recreation or opportunities for engaging with neighbors, and so on. Each of these smaller ends-in-view occurs long before we might set our sights on building a public park as our larger object of hope.

Learning How to Hope. Sarah M. Stitzlein, Oxford University Press (2020). © Oxford University Press.
DOI: 10.1093/oso/9780190062651.001.0001

Objects and objectives are what we hope for in our lives, our communities, and our democratic nation.

Hoping Together

To delineate how we may hope together, let's begin with five approaches described by philosopher Titus Stahl.[198] First, he presents "distributively shared hope" (1), where each individual in a group hopes for something. Even though they hope for different things, they share the property of hoping. Second, he describes "minimally shared hope" (2), where every person in a group hopes for the same thing, but may not know that the others also hope for that thing or may not approve of them doing so. While these are potential starting points to hoping as I see it, they aren't sustainable because they don't provide a climate that acknowledges and supports hope or a disposition to exert effort in the face of struggle. They can also fall prey to some of the problems of privatized hope that I discussed in chapter 1, preventing the effective identification of social problems and the collective work needed to address them. Focusing on these versions of hope might help individuals personally or for a short while, but they aren't likely to bring about the significant and lasting improvements in our lives or in democracy that hoping together can. These approaches also fail to recognize that working with others on problems that hinder our own personal futures is a way to improve our own prospects as well as those of others. We need forms of hope that better link one's future possibilities to the well-being of the country as a whole.

Third, Stahl describes "cooperatively shared hope" (3), where each member of a group hopes for some thing and is aware of and supportive of the others also hoping for other things. This form of hoping together is the minimum foundation for which I am calling. Here, people are enacting hope and acknowledging the importance of others who are also enacting hope, even if their particular objects or objectives may vary.

Fourth is "fully shared hope" (4), where each member of a group knows about and supports each other in hoping for the same collective outcome. And fifth is "collective hope" (5), where all members of a group jointly hope for the same collective outcome. In this case, "the group acts on joint commitments, but each individual also has derivative commitments from the group that are distinct from their own personal commitments.[199] Both 4 and 5 are more desirable for the overall well-being of democracy because they entail not just the practice of each individual citizen hoping, but also those citizens hoping separately or together for some outcome that is mutually beneficial. When those outcomes are public goods or conditions that lead to the flourishing of collective life, the shared content and hopers are brought together in a situation that is particularly ripe for reviving democracy. Options 4 and, especially, 5 may also involve creating an imaginative space where members creatively work together toward their collective outcome. Such a space not only can generate new ideas but also can be a sandbox for experiments in shared living, where citizens are mutually recognized and no one feels left behind or slighted. Versions 4 and 5 also differ from privatized hope; they entail us inviting others into our hoping action, potentially revealing the sources of problems, and providing a space for social problem-solving. These options assert the value and importance of shared and collective work. Let's consider how 3, 4, and 5 might play out as hoping together.

When hope is understood as pragmatist habits, with their deep connections to social and political life, hope transitions from the individual to the community. Hoping involves reflection, action, and consequences that concern and impact other people in one's environment. Hoping together is a process that is more than just the sum of each individual's hope; rather, hoping together takes place in a community that shapes the objects and practices of hoping. Hoping together may start with or build off of the particular hopes of individuals, but through dialogue they become collectively held when others also desire them and are willing to work toward them.[200] Each individual may hold the same object of hope, as in minimally shared hope (2), but may be unaware that others are concerned with the same object of hope. Thus, they feel no affiliation to others as a result. Here, we have a mere aggregation, a summing up of each individual's hope, rather than an association of hopers. This gives us only a superficial identity as merely being concerned with the same object and fails to provide the richer social identity needed to bind people together in America through times of struggle. However, when we hold a joint commitment to that object, it binds us with others, and in some cases, we cannot dissolve that commitment without the community's agreement. This sort of hoping together provides a more substantial sense of social unity.

In hoping together, the community becomes a source for hoping, producing indeterminate situations and shared experiences that trigger inquiry and imagination. And the community becomes a concrete location for hoping, where the people around us influence our attitudes, emotions, and actions. Sometimes we build solidarity by sharing our similar experiences and reactions. Within the community, we identify shared social problems as well as individual struggles, all the while discussing why they are problems worthy of address. We then craft desired outcomes, keeping in mind what we find to be feasible, all the while maintaining a spirit of possibility. In many cases, we work together through the process of inquiry to imaginatively propose solutions to those problems. We then try out those hypotheses together, seeking to determine whether they have increased our ability to lead flourishing lives so that we can grow as individuals and together. When our hypotheses fail, we must come together to deliberate, to seek out alternative views and ideas from beyond our initial community, and to once again creatively envision new approaches to try. With each reiteration, we shape our new objects and objectives critically, checking to see whether evidence supports them and whether they reflect what we truly want or need.[201]

Hope matters to democracy because shared hoping, and the content of such hope, ties communities together. Hoping with others for the same objects and objectives entails a joint commitment that binds us beyond being a "we" of hopers. It gives our connections substance and direction. Hoping together can help support an individual's persistence in pursuing a goal because it enhances our obligations to others and our reasons to pursue the object or objective. As a result of being connected to other people and to shared ends, this hoping together is more sustainable than individual hope because it entails more resources for problem-solving and persistence.[202] It may also nurture our sense of responsibility to follow through on our commitments to those we hope with. Finally, the experience of solidarity can affirm the worthwhileness of action with others and move us beyond more fleeting individualized hope undertaken without regard for others. While despair often isolates us and cynicism distances us from each other, hope builds solidarity in one's commitment to and interaction with other citizens. Commitment to each other and action on each other's behalf builds the trust and involvement entailed in self-government necessary for democracy to thrive.

The practice of hoping together and determining the content of our significant shared hopes shapes our identity; it becomes who we are and how we see ourselves. And when that identity is geared toward future-driven action and betterment of our collective living, that identity leads us to work together as a public. As a result, hope is not just instrumentally useful because it is aligned with specific outcomes but also is intrinsically valuable in constituting our identity. In such a community, our habits of hope are nurtured to keep us disposed toward hopeful action even as our ends-in-view vary. This proclivity keeps us adaptive to novel situations and actively seeking new and better ways of living. Our community is also strengthened when its members understand themselves in terms not only of their shared commitments and aims but also as hopers—as the type of people who flexibly adapt to challenging situations and engage in effort to improve them. Such an identity can help to unify citizens from an array of demographic backgrounds, political parties, and experiences. Even if the content of our hopes differs significantly or we believe that others are mistaken about their vision of a better future, perhaps some of our divisions can be at least partially mitigated by recognizing the shared role of hope in our lives and our shared identity as hopers.

William James was clear that pragmatism "does not stand for any special results. It is a method only."[203] As such, the emphasis should remain on the action, methods of inquiry, and proclivities of hoping.[204] Indeed, it is these practices that sustain our commitment and enable us to achieve the content of our hoping, whatever that may be. Shared hoping binds us together and adapts us to our changing environment. Through hoping together, we build our resolve and bolster our courage to improve the world. When we face disappointment, obstacles, and failures, our fellow hopers buoy us.

Inviting others to engage in the imaginative parts of hope may help break down some walls between citizens prevalent in our currently polarized society. Part of our polarization stems from stereotypes of competing political parties, such as assumptions that Republicans are racist or uneducated and Democrats are elitist and out of touch with reality. When we imagine and problem-solve with others across party lines, we have firsthand experiences that may confront those stereotypes with examples of intelligence, care, creativity, resourcefulness, and more. When we do this sort of work together and our focus is on our shared fate in the future, we are pushed to see the humanity and value of those we may disagree with politically. This may enable us to set aside those differences, even if only temporarily or partially, and perhaps put first the strong collective identity of doing common work together.

Working together also helps us build our trust in the intentions and capabilities of our fellow citizens. We may see firsthand that those different from us can exert effort in the world and can have positive impact that benefits themselves and others, including ourselves. Moreover, we may recognize our own limitations in achieving our goals and come to enlist or rely on others to help us, or we may recognize that a particular problem requires an "all hands on deck" approach. Unlike the self-segregation and echo chambers that many citizens seek today to shore up themselves with only like-minded people, when we hope with others who differ from us, we open ourselves up to them. This may create a space for new relationships and learning across differences. Those relationships may then lead to further identification of shared problems and new endeavors of hope.

Ultimately, the process of hoping with others is important to reviving democracy because it binds us with them, pushes us to take action together to solve our shared problems, and builds an identity based on hopeful effort and commitment to common work. Working across differences can help to combat increasing disengagement and distrust. It can help us confront despair and offer a pathway out of that state, thereby releasing us from paralysis. Such hoping creates and improves some of the conditions needed for democracy to thrive that have struggled most in recent years. As social and political, hoping is a practice immersed in webs of power, where power varies in form, degree, and impact among the people hoping together. And the goals of hope are often shaped by power structures and inequities. Whereas viewing hope as individualist or confined to one's emotions or spiritual beliefs hides power and inequities at play, pragmatist hope enables such power to be better identified, harnessed, and challenged in varying circumstances according to what is needed for citizens to flourish.

Objects and Objectives of Hoping Together

For Dewey, the overarching goal of hoping is a democratic society that supports the growth of individuals and flourishing life for all. He does not describe individual citizens as pursuing this goal explicitly or directly in particular ways, but rather as a spirit that guides our action and reflection so that we are alert to opportunities where we can improve democratic living.[205] It focuses our activities by employing our intelligence to clarify and direct our desires and using our imagination to help us construct means to pursue them.[206] Shade describes this process well:

> Committing to a hope indicates our willingness to promote actively, in whatever way we can, realization of its end. Because it is not within our reach, some degree of patience is needed. But in hoping, patience is coupled

with an active orientation toward the end, an orientation which includes acting *as if*—testing our beliefs about the end and its means—to see what we can contribute to its determination.[207]

Here he brings together the act of hoping via habits and inquiry with the content of such hoping.

Our shared conditions, including the current problems faced in America that I've noted throughout this book, can give rise to shared objects and objectives of hoping. Those shared ends may be for the things and practices of democracy, whether those be formal principles such as justice and equality, things such as public libraries and schools, or ways of life that support and engage democratic living, such as cooperation and deliberation. They may also be values, like respect for persons, and practices, such as listening. They may also be small and specific outcomes a community needs to satisfy some need or solve a problem. Citizens work together to determine that those objects and objectives are realizable and desirable (in that they fulfill present needs but also do not block other, perhaps larger, aims).[208] When the shared hopes arise from people, publics form where people work together to solve social problems and achieve common goals. The content of such hoping comes to compose a vision of our shared life together within American democracy, one that springs from the people and is enacted by them, and one that is, importantly, revisable.

While obvious to many, it needs to be said that not all publics can fairly pursue or achieve their objects of desire due to power imbalances, white supremacy, and more. Some communities have more resources and more cultural and political capital to bring their objects of hope into fruition. A country that substantially celebrates the role of hope would recognize the need to level the playing field so that all publics can more fairly pursue their desired aims. That is not to say it would guarantee their desired outcomes. But at the very least, elected officials could use the sway of their offices to seek out, listen to, and support the efforts and aims of minority, underprivileged, or marginalized groups. In this way, they could affirm, when appropriate, the legitimacy of the problems identified by those groups and bring additional resources, attention, and people power to bear on them, thereby supporting hoping and objects of hope.

A pragmatist is always leery of narrowly defining the shared content of hoping in advance, for it would not arise out of real conditions, inquiry, and the changing needs of citizens. And objects and objectives that do arise should always be held tentatively, open to criticism and revision as needs and environments change. Those objects and objectives should be assessed to make sure that they "work for us" and help our lives flourish without harming others and, ideally, bring benefits to others. Even democratic principles should not be held as unchanging dogma, but rather can only be reasonable and responsible when subject to revision.[209] With that in mind, I will only briefly note here some of the shared content of hoping that might arise in light of our current struggles. These include: a healthy economy, gainful employment, healing of political divisiveness, trustworthy media, and consistent demonstration that each individual has equal value in our society.

While objects and objectives of hopes must be fluid, resulting from deliberations together and inquiry into our environment, there are some elements of democratic life that have stood the tests of ongoing experimentation and remained significant to ensuring the flourishing of American people and may be worthy to continue. These include: liberty, justice, opportunity, tolerance of an array of lifestyles that do not harm others, reduction of suffering, a system of checks and balances that prevents abuses of power, and citizens viewing each other as political equals entitled to the same civil participation, rights, and responsibilities. Often those ends are best achieved or sustained through democratic means: inclusion, participation, compassion, deliberation, and access to citizenship education that prepares one to be an active and effective citizen.

Some of these democratic ideals have long been wrapped up with practices of white supremacy that have denied those ideals to many Americans of color. Moreover, many of those democratic ideals were crafted and determined by only a sliver of the population, namely propertied white men, and therefore not only lack the voice and input of others but also fail to encapsulate the experiences of those for whom the founding ideals have rarely been achievable or equitably provided. Those objects of hope, then, have been shaped by agendas of power that must be acknowledged, analyzed, called out, and challenged when needed. I am not suggesting that we just need to work harder at providing or ensuring those long-standing objects and objectives of democracy, but rather that we need to recognize their connections to injustice and rework them in broader and more inclusive practices as part of our hoping. But I'm also urging citizens to consider how some of these ideals have sometimes served us well in the past and how they can be revised and improved to continue to serve us well now and in the future. Note that some of these are enshrined in the Constitution and yet the Constitution has flexibility so that we can continue to revise how democratic principles and practices look as our environment changes.

Throughout history, the American ideal premised on principles of equality, rights, and opportunities has guided and reunited America through troubling times, such as Abraham Lincoln's invocation of it during the Gettysburg Address. Indeed, following the war, some of our citizens and leaders recognized the need to revise the Constitution to further ensure those principles through new amendments aimed to provide equality to former slaves. And today, frustrated citizens who feel that they are denied equality (because of racism and a host of other things) or opportunity (due to lack of upward economic mobility) should come forward to reassert their importance. They can show the ways those ideals have been distorted by racism and other forms of injustice. For example, concerns with equality for many people of color have been less about receiving resources from the state and more about how racism has systematically led others not to recognize them as persons worthy of equal respect, yet many whites struggle to see this, sometimes choosing to focus on supposedly unjust distributions of welfare, affirmative action, and other state programs that aim to distribute goods rather than acknowledge practices of moral disregard between citizens. Citizens might then expose when those ideals have been contradicted by competing actions, and work toward their improvement, rather than become complacent or throw in the towel on the American experiment out of a sense of disillusionment with its ideals.[210] Such expectations should not fall only on citizens of color and others who are struggling, but also those who are well served currently. Through inclusive listening and inquiry, they should also identify and act on those problems and shortcomings of our ideals.

The importance of America's guiding principles was recently reasserted in the final letter written by Senator John McCain to America. In the midst of an environment where many Americans have bred hatred by reducing patriotism to exclusive acts of culture, he reminded his peers that those principles can bring sustainable happiness and argued that we should turn to them now. In his final lines, he entreated, "Do not despair of our present difficulties. We believe always in the promise and greatness of America because nothing is inevitable here."[211] While pessimism may make bad outcomes seem inevitable, McCain asserted the power of our effort and our employment of the guiding principles that have been central to the promise of our country and its ability to be refashioned.

Shared objects and objectives of hope may help us build a new conception of America that we can rally around—a sense of who we are and what we stand for that we can take pride in, defend, and advance. This may be hard to imagine within such a politically divisive society, but surely there is content to our hopes and our shared fate that we can identify or create together. And some of that content may already be well established within our history, principles, laws, and cultural practices, even if it has become more hidden or has not been fairly distributed in past and recent times. Some of the primary values held by members of certain political parties or civil groups may conflict with the shared hopes of the larger citizenry. Indeed, we can celebrate such conflicts as part of living in a democracy that enables a diversity of views and the freedom to pursue them. But our task is figuring out how to enable all citizens to balance those conflicts while still pursuing their own version of the good life and shared well-being. In part, that requires focusing on the overarching needs and unity of our country as we determine and pursue our objects and objectives of hope.

And, while the continual creation of shared hopes via flexible habits suggests the need for adaptability in one's political views, I recognize that some citizens hold strong views and their ideologies fixedly. While that approach may not be as conducive to a flourishing democracy that is responding to changing needs and environments, I recognize that our democracy has a long history of valuing tolerance, including tolerance of those whose views are fixed.[212] Again, we must work together to figure out how to balance those fixed minority views within a wider society that is flexible, all the while demonstrating the benefits of adaptability and the unifying practice of discussion and engagement with each other. Perhaps we might harness strong views to push and challenge our more flexible ones in productive ways, as we stop to try to listen to and understand the beliefs that some citizens adhere to so tightly. Through such listening and adaptability, we might also model ways that our staunch peers may come to question or change their views in time.

Considering how shared content relates to hoping is worthwhile and may indicate things, values, and ways of living that educators and institutions might specifically nurture in citizens. That shared content may then guide us in our future choices and actions so that we continue to enable individuals and groups to actualize their hopes down the road.[213] And shared content may mutually reinforce the solidarity of hoping together I described earlier. Philosopher Adam Kadlac explains, solidarity seems to require a measure of specificity in the goal being pursued, since genuine solidarity is more than a vague togetherness. It is most clearly present when we face challenges together with others as we work toward something we all care about: winning the game; defeating the enemy; fighting poverty, oppression, and disease. As a result, the content of our hope matters and we are able to develop greater solidarity with those who want the same future as we do and who are motivated to work toward bringing that future about.[214]

I'm also reminded of Bill Clinton's claim that "priorities without a clear plan of action are just empty words."[215] The content of our hopes, then, may be goals, values, and ways of life, but they cannot be separated from our actions to realize and sustain them. Those actions play out as the effort, imagination, inquiry, and experimentation that is hoping. How we hope and what we hope go hand-in-hand, and both matter to democracy.

Democracy Supports Hope/Hope Supports Democracy

Democracy and hope have a reciprocal relationship where each supports the other. Democracy in our republic is aligned with the spirit of change that enables hope for new and different things and ways of life. Our democracy enables peaceful and frequent transitions of power, which not only help to prevent violent revolutions but also provide formal conditions for change. The ability to run for elected office allows one to take a guiding role in shaping government, society, and daily life. With each election cycle, there is the opportunity for new leadership and new ideas to come into power and, at minimum, for current leadership to be reassessed and alternative ideas to be discussed during the campaign season. Those conversations open the sort of space where the inquiry, imagination, and experimentation of hope are fostered at both local and national levels. For example, during the 2016 presidential election, Bernie Sanders introduced some rather radical new ideas regarding free college tuition and universal healthcare in America. While ambitious and difficult to achieve, these ideas generated discussions among citizens. Supporters greeted the proposals with a spirit of possibility and began to imagine how those ideas might look as actual policies, while others criticized their desirability and exposed constraints on their feasibility. Both were important to the process of hoping together.[216] One woman who was inspired by his platform, Alexandria Ocasio-Cortez joined Sanders's staff. Then fueled by passion for Medicare for all, she developed and expanded her own platform, which attracted considerable support. She went on to a surprising upset over a longtime congressman in New York in 2018, exhibiting how hoping and objects of hope can continue and expand well beyond one presidential candidate or election.[217]

Democracy is designed to prevent ideas and ways of life from being crystalized as dogma; rather, they are always open for discussion and challenge, at the very least, during elections.[218] Unlike other some other forms of government, our frequent elections allow us opportunities to reevaluate our priorities and our leadership as our needs and desires change from one election season to the next. Citizens who increasingly champion authoritarian or military rule today may feel currently aligned with the aims and approaches of such rule, but perhaps have lost sight of how our democracy's frequent elections offer opportunities for reassessment and realignment when such leadership no longer reflects the will or needs of the people. In other words, while authoritarian leadership may suit them well now, those citizens are overlooking the benefits of changing leaders offered within a representative democracy. Moreover, those alternative leadership styles squelch spaces for expressing dissatisfaction and imagining improved approaches, thereby inhibiting hope. Given that military rule is supported more by citizens with less education, it may be important for schools and communities to more strongly affirm these benefits of democracy, including through the use of historical examples that demonstrate the benefits of democracy for ordinary Americans.[219] Military and authoritarian leadership arrangements may seem appealing when hope is low or when one is seeking security and order, but they limit the ability to enact hope and restrict peaceful ways of proposing changes in the future, which may actually breed resentment and disorder in response.

Some long-standing democratic conditions and principles bolster hope because they enable the creative pursuit of one's desired life through providing the freedom and power needed to pursue that life without the hindrance of dictators or unwarranted constraints on liberty. The laws and institutions of the state (including schools) can help protect and ensure those conditions of liberty, equality, and justice that are conducive to hope. But it can be hard to have faith in the principles and institutions of democracy when they have failed in the past, when participating in them has been out of reach, or when they appear increasingly controlled by political and economic elites. As a result, it is worthwhile to turn our attention to hoping together and to build resolve by studying the stories of successful efforts of social movements and organizations.

Civil society provides what Peter Berger calls "the plausibility structure" for hope.[220] Civil society, with its clubs and groups, is composed of people who can identify shared problems and exert collective effort to alleviate them. It provides tools, including networks of people, histories of past success of "average Joes," and more, that motivate and make it feasible for individuals and groups to pursue hoping and to fulfill the content of their hopes. In the midst of the increasing privatization of hope, civil society offers a space where citizens can try out hoping together and experience how shared hoping can foster one's habits of hope and the flourishing of the group.[221]

Finally, within accounts of democracy, we often find beliefs that bolster our practice of hoping, such as the belief that the system can ensure the freedom of individuals, provide political equality, and offer opportunities for meaningful participation.[222] In other words, democracy promises desirable outcomes that may motivate us to work toward them and, when achieved, those outcomes are often, in turn, supportive of hopeful endeavors. Democracy is appealing because it aims to treat each person as equal to every other, despite their many differences. That political equality provides a more level playing field for pursuing our hopes, even if our personal hopes may be hindered by other factors such as poverty. When that equality is not achieved, habits of hope kick in to help us identify and speak out against practices that inhibit it and to envision better ways of achieving it. When that equality is achieved, we have greater justification for continuing to enact our habits of hope because we believe there is a fair opportunity for us to pursue our desires. As more Americans increasingly support autocratic and military rule, it is worthwhile to showcase the benefits of democracy here. It enables the conditions for a freer and imaginative space of shared hoping, which can pull us out of despair and improve our lives.

At the same time, hope also supports democracy. Both the practice of hoping, which unites citizens in public work, and the content of hoping, which sometimes is aligned with democratic aims or public goods, engage and enhance democracy. Sometimes hoping brings together diverse groups of citizens, requiring deliberation that breaks down boundaries and builds a sense of *e pluribus unum*. Citizens inquire and experiment together, leading to the discovery of new, more efficient, and more effective ways of living together in our growing country. Because democracy often provides conditions for hope, enacting hope can affirm our commitment to and appreciation of democracy. Pursuing our hopes can also lead to adapting the practices and principles of democracy to meet new situations and needs, demonstrating the flexibility and usefulness of this governmental structure and way of life. Hope also gives citizens democratic resolve, and persistence to withstand the many types of struggles that democracy faces without foregoing the formal or cultural components of democracy.

Being hopeful, though, doesn't necessarily mean being happy with all aspects of our democracy or having a rosy demeanor overall. One can still hope, even when deeply frustrated by the way things are. Perhaps counterintuitively, "Hope often creates discontent, inasmuch as a person's hopes for the future may make them very dissatisfied with things as they are presently."[223] Envisioning possibility can lead us to helpfully critique current constraints on those possibilities. In Dewey's words, "a sense of possibilities that are unrealized and that might be realized are, when they are put in contrast with actual conditions, the most penetrating 'criticism' of the latter that can be made. It is by a sense of possibilities opening before us that we become aware of constrictions that hem us in and of burdens that oppress."[224] That discontent can be used proactively as democratic dissent, which can lead to improvement in the formal structures and culture of democracy. In dissenting, one expresses dissatisfaction with the current state of affairs, helps others to see the problem, and then puts forward solutions for discussion and testing. This discontent becomes an important part of cultural criticism, critique, and inquiry geared toward improving social living.

Unlike cynicism, which fails to suggest solutions for the source of frustration, hope-based dissent mobilizes action and engages democracy to imagine and work toward a better future with knowledge of the past and previous fulfilled visions. In similar spirit, philosopher Michael Walzer adds, "[Criticism] is founded in hope; it cannot be carried on without some sense of historical possibility."[225] It is sometimes those who are most frustrated with the world as it is that, through their scathing depictions of that world, provoke hoping in themselves and others that ignites alternatives. As they do, some of the most effective dissenters recount stories of previous dissent that has led to positive change, thereby bolstering hope and suggesting possibility for our actions now.

Importantly, hoping can occasionally resist elements of change and reassert past ways of life that are being left behind back into the vision of the future. Often, however, dissent is important to a healthy democracy because it generates conversation about the typical ways of doing things and provokes change when those standard ways are no longer effective or when they cause harm to some group.[226] Dissent works against stagnation by bringing forward new ideas and more perspectives on an issue. Our democracy requires the consent of the governed. In order for the laws and practices of a democracy to be upheld, they must be found legitimate by the citizens so that those citizens can consent to them. Through dissent, we expose laws and practices to be illegitimate, out of line with the needs of our society, unjust, or otherwise unacceptable. It then propels us into better ways of living by suggesting alternatives to replace the problematic laws and practices.

One recent example of this sort of dissent is the #MeToo movement, which began by women sharing traumatic stories of suffering caused by sexual harassment and assault, including some stories of being in despair as a result.[227] While crafting a vision of equality and safety for all people, especially in the workplace, #MeToo raised awareness of the pervasiveness of the problem, and encouraged people to share and discuss their related experiences. Consequently, both structural and cultural changes have taken place. New bills to ensure protection and due process have been passed in states and workplaces, new worksite trainings have been instituted about sexual harassment, and the larger population has a new understanding of the pervasiveness of sexual assault and inequity. Even in schools, approximately 14% of surveyed teachers reported changes to their professional development, curriculum, and classroom discussions in response to #MeToo.[228] Many Americans have joined in the hope for making our streets and workplaces safer and more just for all, an aim aligned with equality and opportunity in our society.[229] Most recently, the movement has shifted toward providing resources for survivors and focusing on stories of how people have coped with trauma and moved forward.[230]

Many citizens in America are deeply troubled by aspects of their lives and our society, especially by economic struggles and feelings of being cheated or left behind by others.[231] Despair sometimes manifests as wallowing in those troubles, driven deeper down by experiencing them as overwhelming and perhaps unalterable. The only possible solution may seem to be turning those problems over to messianic leaders or strongman rulers who claim to have simple solutions. But a messianic leader carries the weight of others' expectations of being saved and a strongman leader focuses on what he is going to do for us, rather than drawing attention to what we might do for ourselves and others. Because of this, such a leader may build individualized hope that we may benefit from his action, but does not build our resolve to participate with others in making life better. And sometimes, a strongman campaigns on the impression that he will fulfill everything desired by others, but once in power, actually focuses on his own narrow agenda. Turning to an authoritarian strongman may be something we resort to when we don't feel personally effective in achieving the world we want; yet, it's another way that we resign our agency and turn over our power to someone else. Instead, dissent is a way to take the struggles and frustrations of our citizens seriously and to give citizens agency in addressing them. Dissent enables those struggling citizens to name problems, call for collective work, and engage in action, rather than resigning to the negativity and paralysis of despair. Hope can spark dissent, which in turn, can lead to inquiry and experimentation that fulfills the objects of hope so that people can flourish once again. This suggests that we should seek leaders who are open and receptive to citizen dissent, not those who squelch it or shy away from it. Those are leaders who invite their critics to the table, try hard to understand their alternative views, and act on them when found worthy.

Practicing dissent and forming publics around problems can lead to building social movements. Whereas many citizens feel unheard by current leaders, or cynical about their ability to influence public life, social movements can showcase citizens' voices and attract the attention of leaders. Being a part of such a movement can reaffirm the power and impact of citizens in democracy (even those who may lack money or connections), especially when that movement is able to demonstrate impact. They can also show participants the power of engaging in imaginative problem-solving and experimentation together.[232]

When citizens engage in such hope and experience meaningful improvement as a result of their effort, their agency grows, they recognize their own political power, and they experience increased confidence that may lead them to ongoing effort. In other words, habits of hope provide us the support structure and intelligent direction that enable us to become agents capable of changing ourselves and our world. Political agency—one's ability to participate in and impact democratic life—not only is important to the functioning of democracy but also is a useful way to counter current complacency, apathy, and cynicism. Many citizens today don't feel that they can participate in or have an impact on political life. But the experience of hoping with others and achieving the objects and objectives of hope can showcase the agency citizens do have and nurture it. Or, in the words of Shade, "the very activity of hoping both requires and enables us to transcend antecedent limitations of agency."[233] Experiencing such transcendence can be an eye-opening moment for citizens, helping them to see themselves, their abilities, and their impact in new ways. It can also shift the characteristics they desire and expectations they hold for political leaders, as they become supporters of and coproducers of hope, rather than proponents of a mere "campaign-style" hope.

The agency of individuals is bound up with that of others, as hope often pushes us into trusting in others, and because one's agency can be enhanced and magnified by others. When individuals are encouraged to connect to the work of others, movements and political force can result. On the other end, we know, via the efficacy principle, that individuals will become demoralized if their efforts consistently don't make a difference. The collective nature of hoping, which engages us in structures of support and civil affiliation, can help to stave off such demoralization and buoy us as we continue to try. Hoping improves democratic living because it cultivates an awareness of mutual dependence and builds desirable attitudes, like trust, toward others. These outcomes are significant for the health of democracy even if the goals of our hope are not achieved.

Another way in which hope supports democracy is through the building of culture and identity. Culture, including democratic culture, is often thought of as in the past—memorialized in traditions and statues. But culture is also about the future for which we hope and the shared identity that results from being a part of that vision and its formation. One of the primary ways that we convey our vision of the future, and thereby build democratic culture and identity, is through storytelling. Stories give us accounts of how problems can be solved and how life can be better. Stories can provide evidence that shows people that when democracy is thriving, each citizen has greater likelihood of achieving equality, liberty, and opportunity, which can then help them achieve their own desired possibilities. Stories can also depict the value of the objects and objectives of hope.

Sometimes we create fictional stories about a future we envision and sometimes we retell true stories of the past. Stories of the past can help us to identify social problems, see how people came together around them, how objectives of hope were crafted, and how they were achieved. For example, stories of African American families during the Reconstruction Era exhibit the significant efforts put forward to achieve quality education as a pathway to greater opportunity on the heels of slavery. For a long time, the stories of many of those involved were unknown by people outside of those communities and yet their narrative of hard work and gradual success sustained ongoing efforts within the community and extended beyond it through trickle-down impact on civil rights initiatives in the mid-twentieth century.[234] Similarly, stories of women's suffrage activism highlighted injustice and shared work toward providing American ideals of opportunity and political equality. These examples showcase the powerful impact of individuals and groups, some of whom lived rather ordinary lives, thereby suggesting, through their telling, that other citizens may see their own potential in a new light today.[235]

As I said earlier, Walt Whitman declared that democracy is "a great word whose history remains unwritten."[236] Part of hoping is writing a new history and future together. That future must reasonably account for past injustices (such as structural inequality, racism, and sexism), attend to current struggles, and make feasible predictions, but, to some extent, it can also transcend and transform them via the alternatives it proposes. The future we construct must remain fluid and revisable. Even as such, a "hope narrative" can sustain and unite us.[237] That narrative may depict shared objects and objectives of hope, perhaps helping us to rally around them, justifying their role in improving our lives, and building our collective resolve to pursue them.

PlaceBase Productions is one interesting example of storytelling. On the heels of the 2016 election, the organization recognized the rifts between rural and urban people, the negative image of rural people, and struggles within rural communities that were significant but often overlooked. PlaceBase Productions reached out to rural communities, inviting residents to tell their stories so that they could share their problems, connect to others, develop pride in their communities, and put forward a vision of a better life together. In some cases, these stories demonstrate moving from despair to hope. Through interviews and story circles, those individual stories are heard and gathered. Eventually they are coalesced into a narrative that is performed as a play within the community, thereby serving as fodder for continued dialogue and action.[238]

Notably, politicians often evoke stories of the America they envision. But unless those stories arise from the expressed visions of citizens themselves or motivate citizens to action as a result, such stories fall short and are not capable of sustaining citizens through difficult times. Stories build on personal and shared imagination to give us illustrations of possibility. But storytelling is not just about telling (this is especially true when it comes to politicians), rather it is also about listening to the needs and experiences of others so that we can reshape and improve our vision for the future in light of their insight. Too often politicians and citizens filter what we hear through our own assumptions or confirm what is heard to fit talking points, thereby failing to truly hear the stories being told.

Although it did not address past injustice, and while it takes a different format than many stories, one example of such a narrative was the 1994 Contract with America. In response to polling data and surveys about the frustrations of the American people, Republican leaders crafted this document to outline the values and vision to which they were committed, as well as an action plan of legislation aimed at fulfilling those goals. It was intended to unify voters around an increasingly widespread conservative spirit and give details about what that spirit might specifically entail and produce. It was widely publicized and many Americans considered it a narrative shaping the country, the laws, and the leadership they sought. It became a rallying point for creating a new culture that preserved elements of the past within its vision for the future, and it called for leaders and citizens to get involved in that future. It shaped their voting and their actions.

Hope also supports democracy by developing our identity. From a pragmatist perspective, our identities are based in our habits, including our habits of hope. A pragmatist understanding of hope urges us to see hope as not merely instrumental toward achieving something else, but rather constitutive of our own identities. Our identities influence how we interpret our past and our future.[239] Enacting habits of hope may then impact how we understand ourselves, how we interpret our part in democracy, and how we act on both. They are "conducive to an increased self-understanding [because] we structure our hopes by reflecting on what it is that we truly want and what is attainable in our lives."[240] Cheshire Calhoun further explains, "Hopers, by contrast, do not treat their hopefully imagined future as merely a strategically rational hypothesis that it might periodically be useful to adopt for planning purposes. Hopers inhabit their hoped for future. Imaginative projection of themselves into the hoped for future is constitutive of the way they pursue their ends."[241] When we form a vision for the future, we come to engage in behaviors aligned with that future, thereby shaping ourselves.

Hope, then, isn't delayed or just perpetually held off toward the future, but rather is of value in the moment. This pragmatist view of hope composes us now, rather than just moving us toward something else. And, over time, our identity—who we are and how we see ourselves—can become that of a hoper, one who engages habits of hope. Such a person is well aligned with the spirit of action and adaptability at the heart of American democracy. Growing and asserting such an identity, as an important part of what it means to be an American, may offer sustainable and flexible support for our struggling country.

Finally, an identity grounded in hope may lead to a more flourishing democracy, in part because of its role in publics. These are at the heart of a vibrant democracy and are in contrast to the "complacent class." Whereas we tend to think of democracies as being composed of a single collection of citizens we call "the public," publics are plural and active subsets of people who rally together around some shared problem or interest. They tend to form when people are united through some similar experience and have a need for their shared elements to be addressed. Dewey explains, "The public consists of all those who are affected by the indirect consequences of transactions to such an extent that it is deemed necessary to have those consequences systematically cared for."[242] These publics openly discuss their shared consequences, often by forming organizations or movements, and by seeking a breadth of perspectives on the issue at hand. There, they name their struggles and chart paths to improvement, sometimes through developing shared content for their hopes. These activities build a sense of belonging and mutual concern that counters the individualism, self-interested behavior, and distancing of cynicism we frequently see today.

It is possible for those publics to develop provincial identities around particular aspects of their local experiences or desires. Or, publics may uphold objects or objectives of hope that conflict with one another. Sometimes those identities or aims clash with our national identity as Americans or with other publics across the country. For example, a growing group of libertarians has formed in New Hampshire, calling themselves "Free Staters." They are seeking to maximize individual liberty and reduce government oversight, laws, and intervention. Their vision of expanded freedom shapes the content of their hopes and the political community they are crafting together. Yet, just to their south, a sizable portion of Massachusetts residents celebrate the role of government oversight and protection in enabling equality, which led them to be the first state to legalize gay marriage in a move to secure equality of state-sanctioned marriage for all residents. These citizens rally around the notion of equality that often competes with liberty in a democracy, where pursuing one's personal freedom may infringe on the rights of others. In such cases of localized conflict, we must try to achieve a justified balance between our provincial affiliations and our larger national setting. Sometimes that means finding points of common ground, perhaps in this case, the freedom to love whomever one chooses. Sometimes that requires turning to the history of compromise and enduring principles within our democracy to model a path forward. Sometimes that entails creating a new story that enables those local groups to coexist peacefully under an overarching American identity that tolerates many different ways of pursuing the good life.

Strengthening democracy by supporting and enhancing scattered and fledgling publics requires deep and ongoing collaboration and communication that works to determine, solve, and implement solutions to problems. To meet their needs, they envision alternative futures and construct public goods, including public things, rather than mere material goods for personal consumption. Such is the work of habits of hope. Hope, then, is much more than a mere feeling or a political slogan. It's relationship with and impact on democracy is significant. Hope matters to democracy. Insofar as habits of hope can be cultivated and nurtured formally through schools and informally within families and civil organizations, they offer a pathway out of current problems that is sustainable and itself deeply hopeful.

Reasons to Hope

In light of the many social and economic problems that are causing widespread cynicism and despair, one may be led to ask, "Are there reasons to hope?" Sometimes this question is posed because people are looking for reasons to take action and some assurance that their action would be productive.[243] This chapter answers affirmatively by drawing attention to the citizens themselves as hopers. When the pragmatist worldview of meliorism shapes our orientation to the world and our actions within it, we can engage in hoping with others in ways that increase our agency, achieve our objects and objectives of hope, and improve our democracy. We are the reason to hope. This is specially the case when our identity is based in hope, as philosophers Claudia Blöser and Titus Stahl explain: "When hopeful activities and attitudes form an essential part of a person's identity, that person has reason to engage in such activities."[244] We have the ability to create and engage hope through our habits. And, as I will explain in the final two chapters, those habits can be taught and learned. We don't have to develop hope on our own and we don't have to go about enacting hope without support. We can nurture the hope of children in schools and develop a larger culture that aids the hope of adults.

5

Teaching Hope, Not Grit

Hope and education are deeply connected. Education itself seems to be a hopeful endeavor insofar as schools are focused on preparing for the future and aim to make that future better than the present.[245] Many people see cultivating hope as an important goal of education, one that sustains graduates through changes and ushers our society into an uncertain future with a positive spirit. While you might expect school administrators and parents to believe that student achievement is the primary indicator of school success, especially within an age of test-based accountability that often overshadows educational aims beyond test scores, 83% of superintendents actually believe that getting children to have hope in the future is a marker of school effectiveness, and 77% of parents agree.[246] Some schools are now labeled "schools of hope"[247] and others are celebrated for the hope they produce in films like *Waiting for Superman* and *The Lottery*.[248] These images of schooling are accompanied by proclamations that " 'Hope is the essence of teaching,' 'To teach is to be full of hope,' and 'Teaching is . . . in every respect a profession of hope.' "[249]

Yet some schools are coming up short. Or, perhaps some schools and teachers are unable to embrace teaching for hope in light of the penalties they face if they divert attention from tested areas. For evidence shows that only half of students say they are hopeful about their ability to succeed in school or other areas of life, while the other half identifies as either "stuck" or "discouraged."[250] Those who are hopeful tend to do better academically, attend school more regularly, overcome obstacles to pursue their goals, and have a positive outlook on the future.[251] People tend to regard most children as essentially hopeful beings. While we know that youth often offer a refreshing outlook on the world and a faith in great opportunities ahead, we certainly know this is not always the case for all children or in all communities, especially for children who have witnessed or been victims of great suffering. In many cases hope is not inherent in the lives or outlooks of children; rather, developing informed and sustainable hope requires education.

Learning How to Hope. Sarah M. Stitzlein, Oxford University Press (2020). © Oxford University Press.
DOI: 10.1093/oso/9780190062651.001.0001

Hope is more than just a political project, as I've largely described it in the chapters so far; it's also an educational one. Beyond correlating with increased academic performance, developing habits of hope can lead to being better citizens because it attunes students to their civil potential, grows their political agency and courage, and enables them to craft visions for our future democracy. Surely, then, teaching pragmatist hope, with its significant implications for social and political life, should be central to citizenship education.

Educating good citizens has been one of the most important and longest held goals for American schools. Extending into recent years, preparing responsible citizens has been the highest or second-highest ranked purpose for schools on the annual Phi Delta Kappa poll, which surveys Americans' views on education issues.[252] And, on a 2013 national Civic Education and Political Engagement Study, 76% of respondents said that schools should be preparing responsible citizens.[253] But other studies paint a more complex and shifting picture of our goals. For example, a 2012 Thomas B. Fordham Institute survey found that respondents strongly believe a high quality core curriculum and an emphasis on STEM (Science, Technology, Engineering, and Mathematics) education are far more critical in schools than instruction in democracy and citizenship, which was found only moderately important.[254] And a 2014 Association for Supervision and Curriculum Development (ASCD) poll, as reported in the blog of an ASCD associate, found the most widely held purpose of education to be "to create learning conditions that enable all children to develop to their fullest potential," followed by, "creating adults who can compete in a global economy."[255] Anecdotally, educating for citizenship is often not at the forefront of many citizens' concerns with schools, and actually may even be contrary to the self-interest and materialist educational goals we see developing today.

While the goal of educating for citizenship persists in some regard, changing understandings of the role of individuals, economic competitiveness, and academic achievement in tested subject areas may be reshaping this long-standing goal both in terms of its value and how we understand its practice. All of this not only suggests the importance of foregrounding teaching for hope but also reveals that the chief location for such teaching to itself be in an increasingly precarious position. While I will focus here on citizenship education as the logical home for teaching hope, I will argue in the next chapter that teaching hope should extend across the curriculum and into cultural and societal practices outside of schools.

In the meantime, I will turn my attention to one seemingly hope-aligned educational approach that has gained some traction in schools, developing grit, to raise concerns with that approach. I expose how grit may relate to or possibly event exacerbate political despair, as it leaves systems of injustice in place and may further frustrate citizens who face them. I show how the individualist and unquestioning focus of grit is not aligned with best practices in citizenship education that are social, deliberative, and engaged with community problems. I then show how learning how to hope may overcome some of the shortfalls of teaching grit. Finally, I ground the teaching of hope within practices that nurture habits of democracy.

Citizenship Education

While teaching hope must extend out into noneducational arms of our society, in order to reach a broader swath of our struggling citizenry, I want to begin by thinking about how we might teach hope within citizenship education. Of course, any discussion of creating good citizens is driven by an underlying view of democracy. Although citizenship is, at root, a status based on the rights and duties of a person within a specific location, we don't have to see citizenship as a mere status. Rather, citizenship is viewed as a normative way of behaving—how one *should* fulfill one's rights and duties in admirable ways aligned with one's conception of democracy. Given my pragmatist, participatory account of democracy, where publics form to work toward common goods and the flourishing of themselves and others, good citizens are those that participate in civil and political life, critique problems in the world, and ameliorate them through hopeful inquiry and action.

Any quality citizenship course aimed at children sufficiently old to appreciate historical differences should entail a careful discussion of how citizenship has differed across time, place, and social position, though I recognize that such discussions rarely occur. If they did, students would see that good citizenship is not something that has been decided once and for all. Students, as developing citizens, should feel some ownership in shaping the meaning of good citizenship. Importantly, though, they bear the responsibility of learning the history that informs the vision they craft.

Citizenship education should prepare children to participate and thrive in social and political life, as it currently exists, including all of the despair and divisiveness we witness today. These struggles should be fodder for classroom discussion and action, rather than ignored or checked at the schoolhouse gate. But citizenship education should also prepare students for a better democracy, including preparing them to improve the current ways of life to move toward that enriched vision. We don't want to merely acculturate children into an existing order; rather, they should question how that order came to be and consider whether there are other, better ways of living. Both to perpetuate and to improve on current democracy require civic knowledge, which has been shown to help students understand how public policy and events affect themselves and others, and civic skills, which have been shown to increase student comfort with political participation and their likelihood to pursue it.[256] Over time, the ways in which we teach children to be citizens have changed, and we have learned that some approaches are better than others for nurturing such knowledge and skills.

For many decades, beginning during the Progressive Era, American schools required civics courses, often with the intention of assimilating new immigrants into American ways of life and affirming those practices for native-born citizens. Those courses were based largely in textbook study and class lectures about how to be politically and civically active. As the years passed, civics focused in on citizens' rights and responsibilities. By the 1950s, civics education was largely conformist in nature, seeking to inculcate obedient and hard-working citizens who would do as expected in order to keep the state stable and secure. To achieve that end, civics courses focused on the tedious details of governmental laws and procedures, which appeared to be part of a well-oiled machine further maintained by a heavy dose of patriotism. Sometimes, especially during war and social upheaval, students were encouraged to unquestioningly support their country and their government, without critiquing or criticizing it. Today, many of those courses have been replaced with general US Government courses that are more likely to describe the details of how government works with little discussion of how the particular student or community might be involved in that process.[257]

The broader term of "citizenship education" seeks to go beyond that twentieth-century view of civics education to consider how one might actually best live one's public and private life in the context of others in one's local, and increasingly global, community. While citizenship education is still concerned with understanding how our government works and how the safety and well-being of our country can be preserved, it extends beyond just the confines of government. It stretches into learning about other sectors where people interact, from churches to online communities. Education for democracy extends even broader, going beyond school walls to teach children about the many ways in which we engage in associated living. While I'm ultimately concerned with that broadest realm, I will confine most of my discussion of teaching for hope to citizenship education. Citizenship education takes place most overtly within schools, typically as part of the social studies curriculum. But it doesn't happen only in schools; rather good citizenship education brings the outside world into the classroom and brings classroom learning to bear out in the real world.

Unfortunately, however, social studies education has been increasingly squeezed from the K-12 curriculum in recent decades, as emphasis has shifted to the more heavily tested areas of math and language arts.[258] Additionally, social studies opportunities vary across demographic groups, with wealthier and white students more likely to receive higher-quality citizenship lessons than other children.[259] When considered in light of recent struggles with despair, which also vary across populations, limited or subpar social studies education opportunities, which nurture hope, may further hinder some students more than others. While I call here for quality citizenship education to teach all students in all locations how to hope, I recognize that evidence already shows considerable inequities in citizenship education opportunities and those disparities must first or simultaneously be ameliorated. Moreover, as we work to cultivate hope, the history of those disparities should itself become fodder for conversation about the presence of despair and injustice.

So, what do we know about the best forms of citizenship education that are offered in schools and how might they shape the way hope should be taught in schools? First, we know that issues-based citizenship education classrooms engage students in a critical and collective setting with real issues in the world around them—social questions and problems that are directly relevant to their lives. The problems are viewed as real and meaningful, and within an inquiry-oriented classroom the approach emphasizes how those issues may be changed and improved by the youth, unlike adults who may increasingly feel like that cannot make a difference in political life today. The inquiry approach aligns with the recommendations of the National Council for Social Studies in their C3 framework. Through such inquiry, students come to "know, analyze, explain, and argue about interdisciplinary challenges in our social world."[260] Students are supported in asking questions about the world around them, gathering the disciplinary knowledge and facts needed to make informed decisions about the problems, exploring supportive and counterevidence, developing confidence in expressing their opinions about the issue, planning a course of action to address the problem (when relevant), and reflecting on their actions and their impact on the world.[261] Each of these steps aligns with how hope is supported and enacted in social groups.

Second, opportunities to express influence over the policies of one's own school can be an especially fruitful approach to citizenship education that simultaneously validates students' voices and knowledge. But these action- and issues-based approaches must be supported by knowledge of government and political theory so that students move past the mere excitement of civic and political action. Such supports can lead to more enduring knowledge of how engagement is best done and why it matters for democracy, enabling students to sustainably continue such acts in the future. Such knowledge guides action with "intentionality, context, and, ultimately, meaning."[262] The results of quality citizenship experiences have positive impacts on both individual and neighborhood social outcomes, including reduced violence and improved health, when citizens have "collective efficacy, which means a habit of taking common action to address issues."[263] Such collective action is well aligned with habits of hope.

Next, from a study of more than 90,000 teenagers, we know that classrooms that encourage respectful discussions of civic and political issues and explicitly focus on learning about voting and elections, produce students with greater civic knowledge, civic engagement, and voting rates.[264] And when those discussions also engage people from different backgrounds and cultures through small group work, reading of diverse literature and news, and forming groups that ensure equitable representation when possible, students build relationships and civil engagement.[265] Such interactions may help confront and overcome divisiveness in our society today.

But, citizenship education should expand not only outward toward others but also inward toward oneself by targeting social and emotional learning.

> Social and emotional learning involves developing the skills needed to recognize and manage emotions, handle conflict constructively, establish positive relationships guided by empathy, engage in perspective-taking, make responsible decisions, and handle challenging situations effectively. . . . When such experiences are well-designed and managed, with space and time for reflection built in, they can support the ongoing development of social-emotional resilience, intellectual agility, and cultural competence.[266]

Recently, many states have shifted toward teaching and measuring aspects of social and emotional learning, partly as a way to move beyond the narrow educational aims of testing only a handful of subject areas.

Of course, these citizenship education approaches also need to be considered relative to trends among the youth population. While it is difficult to gauge many of the changes currently unfolding, especially within younger age ranges, we do see some significant shifts forming from the Millennial Generation (born 1980–1995) to Generation Z (born in 1996 and after) that can help us improve high school and college education. During the 2008 election, many Millennials embraced the "yes we can" spirit of President Obama, leading to dramatic increases in voter turnout.[267] And yet, only a few years later in 2014, youth voting was at record lows, only to rise again in the 2018 midterms—perhaps a sign of significant swings and frustration among Millennials.[268] In recent years, Millennials have continued to see politics as a vehicle for change, but are frustrated that the political system is often inefficient and difficult. Many want to participate, but doubt their impact or aren't sure how to do so.[269] They are also frustrated with the spin of polarized debates, yet they enjoy discussing the nuances of and compromises to difficult situations with their friends. They seek group consensus and collective action and don't want deliberations to get bogged down by competition or other problems that stall action.[270] As a result, some turn away from political activity and prefer only to volunteer occasionally with local groups on issues of personal importance.[271]

It appears that Generation Z, however, is more politically active than the previous generation, even though percentages of actual action are still relatively low. The rise may be linked to certain social protest movements that many youths are leading or participating in, including school walkouts over gun violence, #MeToo in response to sexual harassment and assault, and Black Lives Matter regarding the unjust killings of black people. What seems to be emerging is that this generation is more aware than ever of social and political issues due to the instant access to information provided by the Internet. While Millennials also largely had that access, they were not as mobilized to action. Perhaps this was due to a sense of despair and separation from the issues happening around them—a feeling that they could not make a change and that the outcome would be the same regardless of their involvement. Generation Z is more likely not only to get involved but also to feel that they can make a difference. They are also more motivated to assume leadership positions, with 40% of those polled in 2015 claiming it was "essential" or "very important" to become community leaders and nearly three-quarters saying that helping others is an important goal.[272]

Generation Z appears more committed to helping others, evidence that disputes anecdotes about youth as merely self-centered.[273] Indeed, researchers of one major study of the group concluded that they have a " 'we'-centered mentality, one in which the majority of their concerns center around the well-being of everyone rather than solely themselves."[274] Finally, Generation Z seeks to transform the world around them by pragmatically addressing root problems of issues, rather than just taking on symptoms or simply discussing ideals, as some in previous generations were prone to do. Rather than performing brief volunteer projects, Generation Z members prefer to undertake larger efforts to alleviate the underlying problems leading to the need for volunteers.[275] As a result, project-based learning, which seeks to deeply understand and impact large, cross-disciplinary issues, aligns with the tendencies of Generation Z.[276] Engaging Generation Z in authentic civic experiences while simultaneously giving them tools for effective communication and foundational civic knowledge will likely continue to encourage action, service, and support leadership development.[277]

Distinguishing Teaching Hope from Teaching Grit

In the midst of background talk of hopeful schools and changing generations, emphasis on teaching grit has come to the foreground as another aim of education intended to enable children to pursue their goals and achieve success during and after school. Indeed, some states have identified it as a teachable and measurable component of social and emotional learning. For many parents and citizens, this has been a welcome shift away from narrow adherence to the particulars of tested subject matter and toward larger issues of life and character. Grit has moved from speculative psychological literature and research studies into school practices and policies from major districts like Baltimore City Schools to small schools like Edge Middle School in Texas. In my town alone, I've witnessed "grit" on everything from high school sports team t-shirt logos, to an elementary principal's yearly goal list, to a chest tattoo on a leading school reformer and city councilman.

In addition to the celebration and implementation of grit in many individual schools, recent federal law (Every Student Succeeds Act) now requires all schools to assess at least one nonacademic measurement of social and emotional learning. Grit, believed to be measurable, appeals to some schools and states as a worthy choice. Additionally, students taking the National Assessment of Educational Progress will now also be assessed on their grit.[278] Even teachers have been studied for their grittiness in order to assess their effectiveness and retention.[279] Catching on to the trend, philanthropic education reformers, like the Walton Family Foundation, have pledged millions of dollars to support the study, teaching, and measurement of grit.[280]

I want to briefly discuss this seeming hope-aligned trend of teaching grit in order to differentiate it from pragmatist political hope and reveal some of its shortcomings, including showing how teaching grit does not reflect what we know about quality citizenship education and how it may relate to political despair. As education becomes enmeshed in the discourse of grit, I intend to bring hope out of the background and into focus. While there are marked differences between the two concepts, my intention is not to construct a problematic dualism between the two, for not only is there some value in having grit but also surely there is helpful space where they are informed by one another and crafted into something unique and useful. As such, the notion of hope I offer in this book may be used, at times, to supplement, refine, or improve theories of grit. Or it may be used to supplant theories of grit by suggesting alternative ways forward as we seek visions of educational effectiveness that extend beyond test scores and into the lives of children and the future of American democracy.

To understand grit, including its benefits and drawbacks, I want to begin with a brief summary of its key elements and related aspects of hope, as described by major proponents. It is important to acknowledge that while developed only relatively recently in psychological studies, grit has been picked up in education literature, practice, and policy in myriad ways, sometimes morphing considerably from the ways in which the original researchers understood it. Some of these adaptations, such as measuring its growth in children to evaluate the quality of schools, have raised new concerns about the focus on grit, causing even leading proponents to issue statements of caution regarding how grit is now being used in schools.[281]

Defining Grit

Psychologist Angela Duckworth has made the most noteworthy contributions to the study of grit. For her, grit is not just working hard, but also staying loyal to one's overarching goal for an extended period of time and through all obstacles that might hinder one's path to the goal.[282] That overarching goal is supported by a hierarchy of smaller goals. While one may not stubbornly pursue all of the smaller goals, the overarching goal should be pursued with passion and perseverance. She explains, "What I mean by passion is not just that you have something you care about. What I mean is that you care about that *same* ultimate goal in an abiding, loyal, steady way."[283] Duckworth also appreciates hope insofar as she says it is important at every stage of grit because it helps us persevere as we pursue our goals.[284]

While other proponents of grit and some school applications understand it to be more narrowly tied to goals that are concerned only with oneself, Duckworth acknowledges that many of the grittiest people she has studied claim that the purpose behind their passion and perseverance arises from the fact that their overarching goal benefits others.[285] She also suggests that grit can help one be more "useful" to others.[286]

Using a test originally designed alongside her fellow researchers Chris Peterson and Martin Seligman, Duckworth developed a series of questions designed to measure one's level of grit, which she calls the Grit Scale.[287] Interestingly, her Grit Scale includes measuring the character traits of grit and optimism.[288] Also, she argues that grit can be improved by one's self or by others; in other words, grit can be taught.[289] One way to do this is to engage in deliberative practice, which one should do repetitively until it becomes what most people characteristically think of as a habit.[290] Additionally, surrounding oneself with what she calls a "gritty culture" may enhance the grit of individuals.[291] Finally, developing grit is aided by adopting a growth mindset. As defined by researcher Carol Dweck, a growth mindset is "based on the belief that your basic qualities are things you can cultivate through your efforts."[292] People with a growth mindset "take the challenge, learn from failure, or continue their effort."[293]

KIPP charter schools have adopted Duckworth's vision of goal-setting grit and now measure each student to determine whether s/he has "finished whatever s/he began" and has "stayed committed to goals."[294] Following Duckworth, they pair the measurement of grit with measurements of self-control, including determining whether s/he "remained calm even when criticized," "was polite to adults," "kept temper in check," "followed directions," and "resisted distractions." This focus and self-control even play out in everyday classroom expectations such as SLANT, a physical way of controlling oneself and staying focused on the teacher.[295] Elsewhere, teachers such as

New Hampshire's Amy Lyon, have crafted grit curricula that bring together perseverance, self-control, and optimism.[296] She encourages students to construct their own specific, measurable goals and then to exhibit self-control in devotedly pursuing them.

C. R. Snyder, a leader in positive psychology, made significant advances in theorizing hope. His work has also been picked up in the study of grit due to the many similarities between how grit advocates understand the two terms. I will lay out his contribution and related contributions that followed in order to shed light on the understanding of grit that I will then critique. Like Duckworth, Snyder focuses on a long-term future mapped out through goal-setting. He emphasizes forming one's own specific goals and pursuing them independently. Once those goals are clearly defined, hope acts as the cognitive willpower and waypower to fulfilling them. However unlike hope and the process of inquiry that supports it, Snyder's goal-setting typically demonstrates little regard for the substance of those goals and their consequences for the well-being of others.[297] Much like grit for Duckworth, Snyder's hope moves us forward and increases our agency. Snyder has also developed a Hope Scale, which measures one's cognitive drive and self-confidence. The Hope Scale is primarily focused on one's own agency, without concern for other aspects or people involved in hope, or the impact of one's hoping and goals on other people or the environment.

In similar spirit, educational psychologist Valerie Maholmes ties hope to personal agency and working toward one's goals.[298] Hope becomes a form of action and will, reflected in the adage "Where there's a will, there's a way."[299] Hope is not mere wishful thinking, but rather happens in the development of pathways toward achieving our goals, motivation to act on those goals, and believing that we can be effective in doing so. That cognitive work can produce emotional responses as goals are or are not fulfilled, but the emphasis is on the action and resilience of the mind, demonstrated through adaptation and growth. This accent on the mind is significant, because few psychologists describe their study of grit or hope this way. Education reformers such as Paul Tough often champion grit as a noncognitive aspect of character, juxtaposing it to the cognitive work of demonstrating mastery of tested subject matter.[300]

Another pioneer in the area of positive psychology is Martin Seligman, who focuses primarily on developing optimism through cultivation of cognitive skills. For Seligman, and later for Duckworth, optimists are those who see defeat as not their fault, but rather as a temporary setback that pushes them to try harder, while pessimists see defeat as not only their fault but also likely to endure.[301] He adds, "Finding temporary and specific causes for misfortune is the art of hope. . . . Finding permanent and universal causes for misfortune is the practice of despair."[302] This relates to Dweck's growth mindset, which includes having optimistic ways of responding to adversity. Dweck, in her account of growth mindset, and Duckworth, in her account of grit, both call for optimistic self-talk to help one persevere through adversity.[303] Teachers have operationalized the ideas of all three scholars by encouraging optimism in students through the use of positive language and focusing on what they can control.[304]

Relatedly, Harvard physician Jerome Groopman, drawing closely on the work of psychologist Richard Davidson, extends hope from being simply a cognitive experience of believing one can have control over the world to being an emotional response that can shape our mental understanding. For Davidson, hope, unlike blind optimism that obscures our vision of the world and leads us to only see rosy outcomes, helps us "bring reality into sharp focus."[305] Unlike trends in the educational implications of grit and hope, he describes their shared feature of resilience, not as springing back and carrying on through dogged persistence, but rather as maintaining positive feelings in the face of struggle.[306] Groopman explains that these positive feelings are related to the release of endorphins and enkephalins that block the pain we may experience during physical adversity.

Finally, Paul Stoltz implements ideas about grit in schools, including the High Teach High School in San Diego. He uses "grit" as an acronym that includes "growth (mindset), resilience, instinct, and tenacity." Like other views of grit described so far, his is goal-directed, though more tied to self-beneficial goals. He describes grit as "Your capacity to dig deep, to do whatever it takes—especially struggle, sacrifice, even suffer—to achieve your most worthy goals."[307] While he does claim that good grit entails striving for goals that may help others, the focus should "ideally" be on oneself and then extend outward to benefit others. In a telling example, he notes exercise as primarily serving oneself, but also reducing one's burden on others.[308] This reveals a pretty limited understanding of social benefits, where they are merely a reduction of one's personal burden on others rather than a concerted effort to achieve common goods.

Stoltz argues that gritty education is intended to "fend off the mass wussification (weakening) of kids worldwide"—a sort of "get tough" approach to education that puts the onus on individual children to better themselves and, thereby, society.[309] One's ability to face and overcome adversity using grit is measured by what he calls the "adversity quotient."[310] Schools following the spirit of Stoltz and Duckworth have upheld exemplars of grit, such as Will Smith and Scott Rigsby (double amputee Ironman record holder), who value triumphing over others or over their own physical limitations at all costs.[311] Finally, reflecting this sense of drive, many teachers now only praise students with words that assess one's focus and determination, and some, such as those at Lenox Academy, overtly encourage students to rate and discuss the grit of their peers.[312]

Benefits and Problems of Grit

As grit makes its way from psychological theories to classroom practice, it has rightly drawn our attention to the fact that good education is more than just nurturing intelligence or demonstrating achievement on a test, but rather reaches other aspects of character development, outlook, and ways of being. Emphasizing grit also helps us to see the importance of related traits, such as positivity, perseverance, and tenacity in responding to challenging conditions, with a bent toward continued learning and commitment. It works against anecdotal trends among youth for instant gratification. Finally, it draws attention to personal responsibility and urges children to claim and demonstrate some important aspects of such responsibility.

As grit has made its way into classroom teaching, policy, testing of students, and evaluations of schools and teachers, problems with theories and research on grit are becoming apparent. This may be, in part, because common understanding of grit is too limited to serve as a clear guide for school practice or, especially, as a criterion for school evaluation. Overall, there have not been many studies on how to develop grit. Instead, most suggestions come from self-help style books of suggestions.[313] The studies that have been completed tend to focus on already high-achieving populations. For example, Duckworth speaks most frequently about studying national spelling bee participants and Ivy League and West Point students.[314] Indeed, many of those students come from families of means and Duckworth herself recognizes that grit scores are significantly higher for wealthy students than poor students.[315] And, in some studies, grit has added little to predictions of academic success[316] or creative achievement among children.[317]

Additionally, some results do not show that teaching techniques can improve students' grit[318] or, if it does produce improvement, the results are only short-lived.[319] Others have alleged that Duckworth's studies have exaggerated the impact of grit.[320] Even though there is much that isn't settled about grit, what we can glean from its implications and applications in schools reveals worrisome elements. I will summarize some of those concerns here, in order to later highlight how a pragmatist version of hope helps to supplement the weaknesses of grit or replace it entirely.

Most notably, grit focuses too much on following a respectable path to success, reminiscent of Horatio Alger stories of hard-working boys overcoming poverty and hardship to earn a middle-class way of life. This path is primarily one of doing what you are told and not challenging one's conditions, as evidenced in some of the KIPP measurements of self-control listed earlier. It entails complying with one's larger circumstances such as poverty and lack of opportunity, and persisting to achieve grand future goals within or in spite of those circumstances. Perhaps even focusing on meeting one's goals in a far-off future may be aligned with economic privilege, for impoverished people are often so focused on the daily struggle of meeting basic needs that, to them, a call to prioritize a distant future may seem unfathomable or perhaps even foolish.[321]

Sometimes talk of grit seems to even romanticize struggle, glorifying hardship as a source of or demonstrable location for grit. Surely, we do not want to celebrate the incredible strain of conditions such as racism or poverty nor overlook the persistence that many children have already demonstrated under such strain by suggesting that it hasn't been sufficiently directed toward worthy large goals, especially those that mirror images of middle-class success or academic achievement.[322] Nor do we want grit to be so focused on the achieving of grand goals in a distant and glorious future, such that the present, including the depths of struggle and pain within it, is ignored or downplayed.

Finally, we do not want to support an educational approach that does not encourage or aid students in questioning and challenging injustices in society, but rather, as Ariana Gonzalez Stokas says, "reveals itself as a pedagogy in learning to endure suffering."[323] We want students to examine and challenge the social, economic, and political conditions that support or hinder their success and that of others, not just blindly withstand them, focusing merely on achieving their personal goals despite the obstacles they face. We want an educational experience that teaches children how to be democratic citizens who speak out in dissent against injustice and work to assuage it for the sake of oneself, others, the present, and the future.[324]

All of this leads to a pick-yourself-up-by-the-bootstraps mentality, a well-established practice that sometimes places blame on the victim for not being "gritty enough" and urges him or her to just work harder—ignoring the structural hurdles that are often so significant that they cannot be overcome alone. Stokas chronicles the history and persistence of this mentality well in her article, "A Genealogy of Grit."[325] This worldview locates failure within the character of the child, rather than acknowledge the severity of the conditions faced by that child. It sets up false promises by leading one to believe that demonstration of just the right sort of persistent behavior will result in success, and that one deserves such success. To highlight that mentality, literature on grit tends to celebrate exceptional cases, such as Michael Jordan earning a spot on his high school basketball team after initially being rejected.[326] While such examples can help us see elements of grit, focusing on them sets up struggling students for frustration and blame when they do not achieve what those exceptional folks do. It may also be the case that grit gets picked up later in life by successful people seeking a justification for their success and a rationale for why others have not achieved similarly and therefore don't deserve similar rewards. It can feel good to believe that one has earned one's position through demonstrating grit, rather than acknowledging how other factors, such as wealth or family connections, may have influenced one's success.

While it can be good to wholeheartedly pursue one's individual goals, it's also important to occasionally question those goals to determine their worthiness for oneself and others, including any potential harm that the goals, or their relentless pursuit, may cause. Single-mindedness can provide focus, but it can also limit one's awareness of potentially more fruitful alternative options or the implications of one's efforts. Indeed, the best and most difficult choice may be to abandon one's long-term goal and redirect one's effort elsewhere, rather than doggedly stay the course. For example, some grit curricula encourage students to set goals related to the sports they enjoy. If a student aims to be a state wrestling champion, his goal may require extreme weight loss and lengthy exercise regiments that risk his health and time with his friends and family. He should stop to reconsider the goal when he faces obstacles that reveal he may be causing suffering to himself and others along the way, such as risking serious illness or injury or missing an important family event to attend a wrestling meet. We must be careful that unworthy individual goals are not unjustly emphasized over or inappropriately balanced with the common good of families or communities. Furthermore, in the cases where grit pits individuals with the same or competing goals in competition with each other, problems may be magnified and hopelessness may result.[327] Grit is hard to sustain in tough circumstances, and employing grit doesn't help to change those circumstances to make one's future efforts or those of others easier.

Considering the larger systems of injustice and privilege that work to promote the success of some and thwart the success of others suggests that current understandings of grit may be too individualist. Focusing exclusively on one's individual goals without considering the impact of one's self on the pathways of others doesn't help to change larger systematic injustice or even encourage one to work with others within those systems. Adversity not only may be unworthy of celebration but also may stem from root causes that are too deep for individuals to deal with alone. When individuals then encounter systems of injustice, feel silenced in the face of them, or develop apathy about being able to impact them, political despair may set in. They may fail to see a political will for addressing those problems, hearing instead that they should just keep on trying themselves and that others have managed through hard work. Continuing to emphasize the need of individuals to be gritty may further exacerbate this political despair, cutting off communities of support and precluding the development of social movements aimed at dismantling systems of injustice. Such criticisms of grit are important and they pave the way for considering whether hope may be a better alternative.

Turning to Hope

Pragmatist hope, however, may point us in new, more ethical, and more sustainable directions in education. Hope arises initially through inquiry and problem-solving by exploring and testing opportunities that are presented in indeterminate situations, problematic moments when we are unsure how to proceed. Hope is less tied to the distant goals of grit proponents and more apparent in the everyday moments of not having a clear path before us. Said differently, "for Dewey, hope emerges in the anxiety that occurs when our habitual way of doing things fails."[328] It enables us to live and thrive with uncertainty, change, and complexity, where we expect that our efforts can make a difference in shaping our world.

Most people understand schooling as an orderly march toward some clear goal, whether the mastery of material, a diploma, or preparation for career. Indeed, much of the talk about grit these days is concerned with setting and achieving clear goals in a passionate and driven way. For Duckworth, this typically means setting one goal, such as mastering one particular musical instrument and sticking with it for years, rather than exploring other instruments one may discover along the way or shifting to another extra-curricular activity entirely.[329] For Dewey, however, the trajectory tends to be more complicated and less straightforward, as the realities of life alter our course and cause us to have to form new hypotheses about them and revise our aims. Moreover, moving headlong toward a fixed end may not be desirable, for it may entail a limited or even foreclosed vision of the unpredictable future. Hope moves us forward through inquiry and experimentation as we pursue our complicated trajectory. With each step, we alter our goals and our understandings of ourselves and our world; an approach quite different from that of grit, where one first identifies an overarching goal and systematically breaks it down into smaller goals to be tackled.

Unlike the more sophisticated account of meliorism that bolsters pragmatist habits of hope, common conversations about grit are sometimes tied to rather simplistic and even naive accounts of optimism—celebrating a rosy outlook on the future and believing that things will work out regardless of current circumstances. In the context of Seligman and Duckworth's work, optimism is believing that the causes of one's struggles are temporary and not one's fault.[330] Likewise, Maholmes explains that optimism is the perception that one's goals can be attained with little regard for external hazards or even one's agency in forces that may thwart those goals.[331] Snyder contends that optimists don't need to engage with the messy aspects of real life, but rather should stay focused on their personal goals with little regard for their larger social circumstances.[332]

Finally, hope is distinguished from grit because of its basis in habits. Whereas calls for grit often evoke the image of a lone ranger, setting out to achieve bold goals independently, the pragmatist celebrates hope as a social activity. Through transactions that mold our habits, we continually shape and are shaped by the people around us and our cultural traditions. Hope, unlike grit, is not a mere trait held by individuals, but rather an activity we do in relation to our world and in relation with others. The basis of hope in habits reveals its deeply social and political nature. Insofar as teaching grit is all about homing in on individuals, it is out of step with best practices in citizenship education that unite children with others in deliberation and the tackling of real local issues and community problems. It also falls short on other elements of social and emotional learning that bridge divides between students, help them process their emotional responses to each other, and foster relationships. And, focusing on individuals may provoke political despair by turning attention away from communities of inquiry where pressing social problems are tackled and away from social movements where agency and expressing political dissent about injustice are fostered. Cultivating habits, however, falls well within good approaches to citizenship, develops agency rather than despair, and is situated within larger concerns for the maintenance of democracy.

Pragmatist hope is located within and attentive to the muddy and complex circumstances of our daily lives. Unlike grit, it is not invoked only with one's eye to the future and it requires more reasonable and tempered consideration of one's circumstances. Additionally, while habits of hope are housed within and compose individuals, hope is not individualist in the same ways that grit is. Instead, it extends to the social and plays out most fruitfully there because it is guided by growth, meliorism, and the democratic good, each of which takes into account the well-being of others and our impact on them. It pushes us from exceptional individual pursuit of our most ambitious goals to reflective, collective public work to make the world a better place, which may include speaking out in dissent about unjust circumstances. Rather than putting one's head down or digging in one's heels in the spirit of grit, hope urges reflection, change, and action. Pragmatist hope decouples grit from success, showing that one does not necessarily lead to the other, and then offers a path forward through the recognition that, while success is not assured, action is still worthwhile, especially given its impact on social and democratic life. Grit may help some individuals pursue the future they desire, but it will not sufficiently revive democracy, overcome despair, or sustain, let alone improve, social and political life in America.

Grounding an Alternative to Grit in Habits of Democracy

We often think of democracy as something occurring in far-away places, like state capitols, and carried out by other people, like elected officials. We tend to forget that democracy involves us—our words, our actions, and our daily lives. Democracy is not merely a formal matter—bound up in documents, officials, policies, and procedures—but rather, is a way of life. As such, it requires a formative culture that supports the development of habits that lead us to enact aspects of democracy regularly in our lives.

Schools are a key location where we nurture habits of democratic living in particular. They are places where we learn how to share responsibility, work together, and communicate across differences, for example. Within schools, students watch, imitate, and interact with others, often trying out or responding to the habits that others display. Our norms and traditions related to democracy are inculcated through both direct teaching and the hidden curriculum—those behaviors and beliefs that are conveyed more indirectly by teachers, exchanges with peers, rules within a school, expectations for students, and more.

We nurture democratic habits within schools by providing environments and activities that encourage the use and development of those habits. In other words, students require opportunities to try out democratic habits and experiences that affirm the usefulness and value of those habits. In Dewey's words,

> The development within the young of the attitudes and dispositions necessary to the continuous and progressive life of a society cannot take place by direct conveyance of beliefs, emotions, and knowledge. It takes place through the intermediary of the environment. . . . It is truly educative in its effect in the degree in which an individual shares or participates in some conjoint activity. By doing his share in the associated activity, the individual appropriates the purpose which actuates it, becomes familiar with its methods and subject matters, acquires needed skill, and is saturated with its emotional spirit.[333]

Developing habits of democracy, then, entails immersing students in practices of shared social living where they can see firsthand that those habits serve their needs well.

Through the process of inquiry, we learn to identify and focus on our habits so that we can shape them to meet our needs and the practices of a well-functioning democracy. We must craft authentic situations for students that engage them in inquiry and experimentation as they try out and reflect on their habits. Teachers should draw students' attention to their habits and those of others, analyzing their usefulness and questioning whether they can be revised or improved. For example, a teacher might point out to a student his tendency to interrupt classmates, drawing attention to how this proclivity not only is hurtful to his peers who feel silenced but also denies that student the opportunity to be exposed to and learn from the opinions and experiences of his classmates. This can help the student not only see his habit in a new light but also provide reasons for changing it. Within a school, students can acquire new habits and, through the process of reflective inquiry about themselves and the world around them, they can also question and challenge other habits that may not be serving them well.

In a quotation discussed earlier, Dewey links our individual engagement of democracy via habits with institutions of democracy when he says,

> democracy is a *personal* way of individual life; that it signifies the possession and continual use of certain attitudes, forming personal character and determining desire and purpose in all the relations of life. Instead of thinking of our own dispositions and habits as accommodated to certain institutions we have to learn to think of the latter as expressions, projections and extensions of habitually dominant personal attitudes.[334]

So, we should not view democratic institutions as entities separate from us and to which we must assimilate. Instead, they are extensions of our democratic habits. Therefore, we don't just tangentially influence public institutions, we compose them and shape them through our habits of daily life in democracy. Finally, as a personal way of life, our democratic habits arise from our interactions with others and are kept in check by our conjoint activities with them, even as we practice them independently. This differs from the more individualist focus of grit and privatized hope that I've described elsewhere. The emphasis is on seeing democracy within ourselves and our actions.

Habits of democracy are best developed through actively and directly engaging in democratic practices within civil society and schools, rather than through vague talk about how to be a good citizen when a child is grown. They cannot be deeply instilled by merely imparting pertinent knowledge that must then lie dormant, waiting for relevant circumstances to arise before it may be put to use. I recognize that this is a big task of today's schools, which are seldom able to engage in this sort of active and immersed learning, but I contend that citizenship education must employ democratic means to achieve democratic ends. In this way, rather than merely educating *for* democracy—something to be achieved by graduates at some distant point in time or beyond school walls—Dewey's view of habit formation demands educating *through* democracy.[335] We cannot teach students to see democracy as an admirable end goal while engaging in classroom practices that are, for example, totalitarian. Rather, we must employ means that are aligned with the end, allowing students to engage in collective problem-solving, inclusive communication, and shared governance around real and significant issues as we nurture them into a citizenship role.

We also need to provide opportunities for students to engage with long-standing democratic traditions and ideals. While steering clear of indoctrination, a key aim should be to highlight the benefits of democracy. Students can be introduced and inducted into the American spirit, in part, through stories about how our past efforts have led to social, political, and economic success and well-being for many, though not for all or in all situations. Teachers can help students see how hope has supported our country in past difficult times, and how it has created shared objects and objectives that have moved us forward. Simultaneously, teachers can expose students to examples of how democratic principles (such as equal opportunity) have also supported hope, while still recognizing that those principles have not been carried out in ways that have fairly supported all citizens. While celebrating some aspects of success and progress, teachers must be sure to paint a fuller picture of elements of stagnation and injustice, and invite students to take up the work ahead of adapting or dropping past traditions and ideals in order to better ensure fruitful outcomes for all Americans. The thoughts and habits developed in this process are open to change and influence from students, thereby allowing democracy to transform across time, rather than limiting students to a narrow or predetermined sense of democracy or good citizenship.[336]

Finally, good habits of democracy should be flexible, allowing adaptation for an unknown future. While we cannot know for certain what lies ahead in America, we can develop political agency via the formation of habits of hope that supports a flourishing life and the capacity for improvement. Given this, I will highlight some of the aspects of habits of hope that are most in need of attention or could best fulfill some of our present and short-term future needs. I hope to do so with an eye to the extended future, where those habits may continue to be adapted and used. While there are elements of these habits that may have endured centuries of democracy, my focus is not on general or static habits, but rather flexible and context-specific ones that better prepare students for adapting to new and changing environments. These are habits that can helpfully respond to or counter the current struggles in democracy. In addition to developing new habits, teachers can help students identify habits in need of change, such as cynicism, that have become stagnant and inflexible, thereby paralyzing our agency and hindering democracy. Habits of hope allow us to live with uncertainty and complexity. Hope thrives on flexibility, as it encounters new problems and faces indeterminate situations.

Hope and Habits, Not Grit

In sum, while grit may be popular in educational circles, and suggestive of a forward-driven spirit that may seem like hope, they differ in important ways. Rather than a pick-yourself-up-by-the-bootstraps ideology aligned with achieving one's personal desires, pragmatist hope offers a democratic vision of justice and shared action to improve circumstances instead. It is supported by habits learned through democracy. Whereas grit may provide some useful outcomes for individuals, it does not show the promise for breathing new life into democracy that pragmatist hope does. Nor is teaching grit currently well aligned with best practices in citizenship education[337] or even the tendencies we see developing among Generation Z. Whereas Generation Z exhibits a penchant for political participation, serving others, fixing root causes of problems, and group leadership, teaching grit fails to build off those opportunities and may actually even stifle some of those potentially beneficial tendencies. In the next chapter, I build off this foil of grit to put forward a counterproposal for teaching hope—one that grows out of quality citizenship education techniques, responds to the potential of our younger generation, is based in habits of democracy, and is overtly tied to the overall well-being of our democracy.

6

Learning How to Hope

When schools and civil organizations cultivate habits of hope, students and citizens learn how to hope, which may breathe new life into democracy. In this chapter, I move from a broader discussion of what we know about quality citizenship education and developing trends among our younger generation to looking at how habits related to democracy, in particular, can be taught in schools. This includes a call to develop communities of inquiry, nurture communication and deliberation, foster criticality and dissent, cultivate imagination and storytelling, view citizenship as shared fate, and build trust.

We teach citizens how to hope by cultivating pragmatist habits of hope and we revive democracy by connecting those habits of hope to learning complementary democratic ways of life. We cannot merely choose to have hope or be hopeful; rather, we need mechanisms that allow us to enact and sustain hoping across time, and habits provide those. As institutions intimately connected to democracy and spaces of citizenship formation, schools should be teaching the ways of life that enable and activate hoping within us and among us.

In this chapter I outline some approaches to teaching hope that may be most useful for developing durable and adaptable hope that simultaneously supports democratic life and attends to some of our current struggles. While they grow out of real circumstances, I have made my suggestions broad so that they can be adapted for an array of students, including those from various backgrounds and ages. But, due to the nature of needing more advanced skills of inquiry, understanding of culture, and use of language, some of the suggestions are targeted toward older children in K-12 schools and some even extend into the college classes of adults. Do not let my focus on older students be misunderstood; young children are capable of hoping and, indeed, are at an important age for fostering forms of hope that are sustainable well into the future. Teaching how to hope should not be reserved or held off only for older learners.

We should not view lessons and curriculum aligned with teaching habits of hope as extraneous—like an additional task heaped on top of the content

Learning How to Hope. Sarah M. Stitzlein, Oxford University Press (2020). © Oxford University Press.
DOI: 10.1093/oso/9780190062651.001.0001

knowledge teachers already work hard to impart. Teaching habits of hope can be integrated with other classroom content and activities and can align with other educational goals or curriculum standards. For example, a teacher might select a utopian story to introduce that genre of writing to students, while also using it to engage students in expanding their vision of what might be possible in their worlds, thereby building hope. Many teachers are provided a degree of flexibility in selecting the materials they use to develop writing, reading, and critical thinking skills; teachers should also have such flexibility when teaching habits of hope.

The environment a teacher creates in the classroom is also important to fostering hope. To the greatest extent possible, teachers must ensure that students' basic needs are met in the classroom and that they feel safe so that they can devote the energy and focus that hoping requires. And even though students' home lives may be burdened with daily worries related to poverty and other struggles, and even though they may encounter significant levels of despair among their family and neighbors, schools must strive to provide a supportive space where students can explore possibilities rather than be yoked with disabling constraints. Potential problems may arise when children are encouraged to hope in the classroom yet encounter significant despair at home. As a result, some children may come to see hoping as not genuine or even as naive, thereby driving them away from the practices of their school. Yet, despair at home seems to increase the need for teaching how to hope somewhere else so that students are given opportunities to overcome the limitations of their homes, and school is often the most logical location.

Teachers should avoid negative language—from themselves, students, or others in the classroom—that discourages agency or that doubts the abilities of students. Such talk dissuades action and predisposes students toward negativity and passivity. Alternatively, teachers can support the development of student agency through techniques that highlight positive action and praise the pursuit of possibilities. For example, a teacher may help students chart their own progress over time in traditional subject areas, showing them how homework completion and other efforts lead to increased learning, which may be indicated by test scores or other outcomes. And teachers can attune students to their strengths while helping them address their weaknesses—making students become more cognizant of themselves, their tendencies, and their capacity for change—key aspects of habit development. All the while, teachers can affirm the ability of those students to change themselves and the world by employing a language of possibility that is mobilizing.

Develop Communities of Inquiry

Learning how to hope cannot happen in a vacuum. Rather, teaching hope, like quality citizenship education, requires engaging with real issues and problems. It means starting in the midst of the indeterminate situations and struggles facing students and society. Teaching hope must begin with authentic experiences and concerns. Teachers can creatively bring those problems into the classroom through literature, science experiments, news stories, and more. Or, they can construct learning situations that formulate mini or related examples of the problem right in the classroom, so that students experience them firsthand—such as the famous blue eye/brown eye activity to simulate the experience of prejudice.[338] Aligned with the preferences of Generation Z, those examples should not be mere symptoms of other social matters, but rather should get at root problems or overarching issues that are significant and authentic. That is not to say, however, that young children should be tasked with solving complex or seemingly intractable issues, for the level needs to be age-appropriate, while still having genuine meaning for the children and their lives. That said, we can learn from children already hard at work on significant social problems. For example, twenty-one students ranging from ages nine to nineteen have brought forward a lawsuit claiming that manmade and government-caused climate change threatens their constitutional rights and violates the public trust.[339] Some of their like-minded peers across the country and world are engaging in protests to raise awareness and demand change, while others are actively working to stop or slow climate change through developing new technologies and engaging in conservation techniques.[340] Indeed, these children may model for other citizens the sorts of effort and inquiry needed to tackle large problems and to approach them with hope.

Next, teachers should model inquiry, lead inquiry, and/or engage in inquiry with the students, depending on the situation. That inquiry begins with identifying and naming the problem. This helps to give the problem clearer shape and meaning for the students so that they understand not only what the problem is about but also why it is significant to themselves or their community. Effectively describing a problem often requires obtaining multiple perspectives—seeing how the problem impacts different people, in different places, in different ways. Such rich descriptions may help to pull stakeholders into the inquiry, for it reveals how they are impacted. We live in a society where the tendency is to look out merely for ourselves, rendering us unable to grasp the social aspects of the struggles we face and the common good that may be at stake. In response, teachers can work to emphasize the shared impact of problems and issues, which may develop a public around them.

Those connections are not always straightforward or similar from one person to the next. For example, many communities throughout the United States are currently considering whether to remove Confederate monuments. Many such historical figures are even housed on school land or inscribed in the names of the schools themselves. While such considerations often play out among politicians or in courthouses, many students, teachers, and school communities are impacted by the existence of the monuments and by contemporary responses to them. A teacher might bring these struggles to light for students, perhaps by challenging them to consider whether or not a particular Confederate monument on their own school grounds should remain. To do so, teachers must facilitate difficult conversations about the emotions and history invoked by the monument. At the same time, they must realize that some students may not even initially recognize or understand the significance of such monuments, while others may experience them as signs of respect and pride for Confederate soldiers and Southern history, while still others may experience them as devastating reminders of injustice and harm. Teachers should engage students in discussing the potential problems the monument or its removal poses for them, perhaps stymieing their learning or self-value in some way. The teacher should then encourage the students to gather feedback about how the monument impacts those both in and outside of their immediate school community. Students should work to understand the perspectives and rationales of those stakeholders, not merely collect a tally of proponents for various sides of the issue.

Teachers can demonstrate for students that echo chambers of like-minded perspectives are often insufficient for thoroughly understanding the challenging circumstances of the world. For example, proponents of either "side" of the Confederate monument issue may see opposing views in straightforward and simplistic ways, when they actually have a considerable amount of nuance, history, and cultural meaning to be unpacked. And clearly this particular topic is heavily tainted by the history of white supremacy that teachers may need to carefully reveal for and with students. Good inquiry involves social and emotional learning—beginning with self-reflection, seeking out multiple and conflicting perspectives, listening carefully to try to genuinely understand and, at times, empathize with those views, then collaborating and compromising to determine and achieve a shared or just end.[341]

The teacher may need to invite guest speakers or provide alternative and diverse literature to introduce differing perspectives on the monuments in a classroom that may be relatively homogeneous in its population or views. Engaging directly with outside people who hold opposing opinions through field trips, class speakers, or pen pals may provide opportunities for cross-cultural understanding or even new relationships to form across differences. By carefully listening to others, students would likely encounter significant numbers of stories from other citizens, especially those who may be descendants of those enshrined in the monuments or of those enslaved or killed by the memorialized leaders. As evidenced by testimonies provided during seventeen public hearings at the Charlottesville Blue Ribbon Commission on Race, Memorials, and Public Spaces,[342] those stories would likely expose how Confederate statues, flags, and plaques inhibit the flourishing of all people by establishing a climate where slavery is still celebrated through the commemoration of those who fought for it. As a result, some citizens are made to feel lesser than others, and some are left feeling unable to move forward because harmful and hateful elements of the past are still celebrated.[343] Those harms may outweigh the reasons provided by proponents for supporting the monuments or the harms they would incur by having them removed.[344]

Members of the community of inquiry should talk about what they hope for their community's future and the potential impact of the monuments on that future. They should seek to determine what best enables stakeholders to flourish. They should also practice setting objects and objectives of hope as ends-in-view. It can be difficult to determine which goals are realistic and realizable, so teachers should help students develop criteria for shaping and assessing their goals. In this particular case, an end-in-view might be removing a statue from school grounds, supporting students who feel harmed by a statue that is allowed to remain, moving statues to a museum setting where a fuller picture of their meaning is presented, or replacing narratives of cultural pride tied to such monuments with new stories. Teachers can guide students through determining whether those ends are reasonable, what positive changes and unintended consequences they may bring, and how they might be revised over time as circumstances continue to change.

Students should then be empowered to develop feasible, intelligent plans of action or hypotheses based on their knowledge of history, their concerns for the present, and their anticipated and desired future. The teacher should provide relevant information about formal governmental procedures (such as how to petition for removing a monument) and age-appropriate political theory (such as theories on identity linked to these sorts of cultural markers). The teacher should then aid those students in carrying out their plan, helping them to test and refine it as they go through reflecting on its successes and shortcomings. Teachers should model hoping in cautious ways that are open to validation and criticism through ongoing experimentation. As a result, the students and/or the environment may need to be changed to ensure the well-being of the community or the better future the students envisioned.

Such a community of inquiry creates a space for students to view themselves as active agents and to grow their disposition toward possibility, as opposed to apathy or defeat. They may come to see themselves as having political views about the power and history invoked by the monuments, as well as the know-how to act on those views and to have an impact on their community as a result. In the final stages of inquiry, teachers should engage with students in reflecting on and critiquing their own actions and impact. Sometimes this is best revealed through reflections among the students, and sometimes teachers should demonstrate for students their own impact, showing it back to them. If, for example, the group of students concludes a monument should be removed from the school and decides to do so by reaching out to the local community, pursuing formal democratic processes via the school board or local ordinances, and more, the teacher should summarize those actions and their resulting impact for the students. Perhaps the teacher might also showcase them in a school newsletter or through a local media outlet. Such actions can foster feelings of agency—a sense of "we did it!"—attracting students to undertake similar shared work in the future. This affirms and strengthens habits of hope. Seeing hope change the world, changes us.

The teacher might also inform students about similar actions taken by students elsewhere to further bolster their sense of possibility and perhaps encourage them to join their community with others who have similar goals. Additionally, citizenship education scholar Meira Levinson explains that such guided inquiry through action civics work may form a feedback loop, wherein students' actions are affirmed and then repeated.[345] Indeed, students may experience higher self-efficacy—an individual's perceived ability to achieve an outcome, as described by Alfred Bandura—when they witness their own success. This perception then promotes ongoing effort and invocation of habits of hope.

Philosopher Victoria McGeer discusses how parents and peers often grow hope in children, adding an interesting dimension to how we might teach hope. While children certainly can learn some aspects of hope by mimicking the laudable behavior of others, McGeer suggests, "what we find instead are laudable patterns that others see—or prospectively see—in our own. We see ourselves as we might be, and thereby become something like a role model for ourselves. . . . Hopeful scaffolding can therefore serve as a very powerful mechanism for self-regulation and development."[346] Teachers and students might then strive to create such communities that scaffold children to envision and appreciate their own capacities, see themselves as hopers, and to shape their habits accordingly. Such a community is one where hope reinforces its participants, validating their visions of themselves and supporting them as they bring those visions into fruition. It is also a community where children can develop their disposition toward supporting other hopers. For instance, a teacher might describe signs of struggle and frustration or showcase examples in the lives of noteworthy hopers in order to help students identify those moments in their classmates. The students may also be equipped to respond by drawing attention to past successes of the struggling peer, noting strengths or special abilities, and more. Upon recognizing that another is having difficulty, the students may then respond in supportive ways that do not merely entail phrases of encouragement, but rather highlight skills, knowledge, and personality traits of the struggling student to help her see herself anew as she is and might be, thereby discovering courage and persistence within herself to sustain her hoping.

On occasion, communities of inquiry can be improved through exposing students to exemplars of hoping—real people or civil groups that have successfully engaged in hoping and have had an impact that bettered their lives or those of others. When teachers invite these role models into the classroom, they should not merely be celebrated as inspiring, though there are certainly worthy reasons for acknowledging such inspiration. Instead, role models should be encouraged to discuss the specifics of their situations, including oppression if applicable, and the habits that supported them in achieving their ends, so that students make personal connections to the models and learn from the struggles the role models faced during their own inquiry and experimentation. Such learning helps students see how hoping can be activated and supported, rather than merely celebrating successes of hope. And direct engagement with local hopers can help students see such a life as within reach for themselves, as opposed to highlighting exceptional individuals elsewhere whose lives and circumstances may feel quite disconnected from those of the students. Teachers can highlight patterns of action and dispositions aligned with hope so that students are aided in identifying and nurturing similar habits in themselves. Focusing on habits of hope may not only attune students to the proclivities they are developing but also help them to differentiate hope as pragmatist habits from grit, more privatized hope, or passive forms of hope like optimism or wishful thinking.

Finally, in the community of inquiry, students can develop a strong collective identity based on working together to improve their lives or those of others. They may then come to feel a sense of belonging with those in the community—a sense of "we" and a feeling of security that they are surrounded by those who know and care about them. Such care is for their experiences and struggles, but also for scaffolding their self-efficacy. And that identity can be one based on being hopers together. Such care and identity can work against the feelings of isolation and being left behind currently experienced by sizable populations of Americans.

Nurture Communication and Deliberation

As hope has become increasingly privatized, it has been relegated to an internal monologue. Yet, hope, as part of vibrant democratic living, is best shared through discussion and deliberation with others about visions of the future and the best ways forward. As a story that we are writing over time, democracy is richest when all voices lend to its telling and craft its future. Finally, discussion and deliberation are central to good citizenship education, for "a large body of research finds that facilitated, planned discussions teach deliberative skills and increase students' knowledge and interest."[347] Yet, only about half of social studies teachers report regularly practicing skills of deliberation, and only a third report providing opportunities to reach decisions in small groups.[348] And some evidence suggests that substantially fewer teachers actually engage students in genuine discussions.[349] Despite that shortfall, Generation Z seems increasingly interested in taking and leading action on social and political issues. Social media and the 24-hour news cycle keep them abreast of world issues, but they need guidance when interpreting competing information and leading others in making wise decisions. Hence, teaching for hope and reviving democracy must emphasize discussion and deliberation to help students know how to acquire and sift through multiple perspectives as they make choices themselves and with others.

Communication is itself a habit. It underlies good democratic living through making common—aiding in building publics and the sense of "we" that comes with them. Communication is also fundamental to Dewey's views of education and democracy. He states that "education consists primarily in transmission through communication. Communication is a process of sharing experience till it becomes a common possession."[350] So, for Dewey, the public nature of education lies in the process of working together to communicate shared experiences and the knowledge that comes from them. Much attention has been drawn to the first part of one of Dewey's most quoted lines from *Democracy and Education*, but look instead at the final clause: "A democracy is more than a form of government; it is primarily a mode of associated living, of conjoint communicated experience."[351] Democracy, then, is a way of life where people come together through communicating shared experiences. It is communication that enables us to make our lives, our experiences, and our ends-in-view common. Communication doesn't just transfer meaning between two people, it is an activity of cooperation that helps to form and enact communities.

Through conjoint communication we generate and share ideas. Located within communities of inquiry addressing shared problems, these ideas may be articulations of frustration, experiences of suffering related to the problem, proposals for change, or plans for action. Or, in Dewey's words, these ideas "are anticipations of possible solutions. They are anticipations of some continuity or connection of an activity and a consequence which has not as yet shown itself."[352] These ideas can lead us out of debilitating ruts, bringing growth and change. Generating and sharing ideas is also essential to a healthy democracy, where knowledge and viewpoints should be free and openly accessible. Dewey adds, "The experience has to be formulated in order to be communicated. To formulate requires getting outside of it, seeing it as another would see it, considering what points of contact it has with the life of another so that it may be got into such form that he can appreciate its meaning."[353] The formulation of experience and the exchange of ideas are central to the act of creating common identities and solving common problems. And efforts to see experiences as others do help us to make those hoping endeavors more inclusive.

Communication is an act of cooperation that forms not only beliefs but also relationships. Unlike recent trends to isolate ourselves among peers and news sources that confirm our beliefs, communication is not an insular process. It should not be constrained by or confined to the group that makes up a public. Rather, communication must be directed outward; we have to seek out new information to confirm and challenge our beliefs. Communicating entails testing our beliefs against those who differ from us—a sort of experimentation that helps us determine whether we've got it right and how our ideas might impact others. Moreover, building relationships and commonality around experiences of problems can help other citizens understand and, at times, empathize with the struggles of others. This is a notable space where we may acknowledge and attend to the suffering of people of color, those left behind in society, and citizens in despair. And when those struggling citizens live in opportunity and civic deserts, teachers may create and open opportunities for social networks and community building that might not otherwise exist. Encountering the difficult experiences of others may also motivate some students with greater power and resources to expand and share those with struggling classmates and, more importantly, disrupt the injustice impacting their classmates.

For Dewey, communication is "the establishment of cooperation in an activity in which there are partners, and in which the activity of each is modified and regulated by partnership."[354] When both interlocutors come together in hoping and thereby share concern for improving life's conditions and for communicating across their differences, it may be helpful, but not necessary, for them to consciously reflect on their habits. When their habits are characterized by openness or are tentatively held, the responses that they make to one another can be sufficient causes for each to modify their respective responses in turn, hence altering themselves to better achieve a fruitful transaction. It follows that, for Dewey, communication "modifies the disposition of both the parties who partake in it."[355] Communication, as a process of making common, changes its participants and the public they constitute as it negotiates new meanings. In today's increasingly fragmented society, developing commonality through communication may help us affirm or build new identities and create improved ways of living together.

Deliberation entails solving problems alongside others through dialogue. It propels citizens to truly listen to and seek input from people different from themselves so that a wise course of action can be chosen. However, Green warns of

American culture's tendency to substitute dismissal, ridicule, and even shouting down others' ideas for democratic dialogue of the kind that would actually allow people to listen to and learn from one another. Our culture fosters these shared bad habits through political talk shows that too often turn into shouting matches, political "debates" in which participants merely repeat "sound bites" and insult one another instead of proposing serious public policies, real-life events and reality-based dramas in which firms and families rely on the courts and adversarial attorneys to resolve their differences instead of talking with one another, and a pervasive popular culture motif in music, television, and movies of treating a willingness to resort to physical violence as the meaning of strength and personal resolve.[356]

Additionally, many Americans choose to wall themselves off from those they perceive to be different or a threat by withdrawing to rural retreats, living in gated suburban communities, confining themselves to locked urban apartments, or seeking ideological alignment in their virtual communities. They shy away from discussion and exchange with others, especially those who may hold different worldviews. These cultural conditions pose a sizable challenge.

Achieving healthy democracy requires openness to different ideas—ideas that may change the way we live and think. Dewey adds, "To cooperate by giving differences a chance to show themselves because of the belief that the expression of difference is not only a right of the other persons but is a means of enriching one's own life-experience, is inherent in the democratic personal way of life."[357] Schools, as spaces that often bring together students of differing backgrounds, can be an important foundational space for shifting our problematic practices around engaging with others, foregrounding the need for inclusive and civil dialogue from an early age and reaffirming it for the adults brought together through school activities. Even though schools too often reflect various forms of segregation along lines of race, class, religion, and more, mandatory attendance and opportunities for intermingling within them suggest that schools may be a more productive space for these sorts of endeavors than when left to optional outlets chosen solely at one's discretion as an adult.

Teachers should strive to provide conditions that spark conversations while modeling and calling for inclusive and transformational communication. This sort of learning is not confined to social studies coursework, but is also ripe for English courses that draw attention to the power and use of language, STEM courses that require the analysis of scientific problems impacting society, and more. Teachers of all subjects can craft environments that require communication while focusing the attention of their students on their effectiveness and inclusiveness so that their communication can be improved for future endeavors. Good communication can become a habit through repeated use as well as environments and teachers who affirm its fruitfulness.

To dialogue effectively, students must learn to explain their ideas and to justify their reasoning orally and in writing. They must also learn to actively listen, to understand the speaker, interpret the speaker's emotions, connect with the experiences another person is sharing, and probe the logic of the ideas offered. Teachers can support students' growth in these areas through small- and large-group discourse. As they facilitate discussions, teachers also model how to respectfully question, clarify, and summarize ideas. In the midst of discussions, teachers can encourage students to pause or to slow the rush to jump in with their own ideas or emotional responses, checking in to see whether others have been genuinely listed to and understood first. Teachers can model the sorts of summarizing and follow-up questions that confirm an interlocutor has been heard and sufficiently understood. They may also use think-alouds to make metacognitive practices transparent.[358] Teachers who prioritize dialogue and written communication improve students' abilities to explain and justify, as well as to express emotion and convey embodied experiences that may be difficult to pin down in words. Students working to jointly solve problems use such skills to define and address problems so that processing of important information is clearer within the group and more persuasive to those outside of the group who may be implored to take action on the problem in some way.

During deliberation, discussions about the abilities of the participants to engage in resulting action should be discussed. In other words, is each individual capable of doing what might be required of him or her in the given course of action proposed? If not, this may be a time to acknowledge one's own limitations and turn to others for help or to scaffold the agency and self-efficacy of others. In the midst of crafting objects and objectives of hope and identifying avenues to pursue them, teachers might encourage the formation of joint commitments that help to not only bind students together but also give their connections substance and direction. Such joint commitments can reveal our obligations to others and remind us of reasons why we should engage in effort to ameliorate problems.

Students may be familiar with decision-making based on a majority vote, but teachers can extend their knowledge around other possible means for choosing a course of action. Using dialogue to uncover the merits of various options may help students creatively combine two or more strong ideas into a new, better option. Another approach may call for the enactment of a compromise with which no one holds strong opposition, asking, "Can we all live with this course of action?" Co-defining the end vision, and what results constitute success, should occur while considering which choice to enact. The end vision is negotiated and refined as students determine what embodies success. Informed decision-making considers not only the best course of action but also the plan that can be accomplished with the resources available and within the commitment level of the group.

Defining success through the process of deliberating about best courses of action also reminds us that failure is a possibility. To curtail an immobilizing sense of future failure, teachers should discuss this possibility with their students, helping them to recognize that commitment and follow-through increase the probability of success in the endeavor. Continuing to act while acknowledging the complexity of the situation and the barriers to success is an important component of pragmatist hope. "Even in situations where groups are defeated, the worthy act of trying to change something that is meaningful sometimes buffers the emotional low that comes from defeat."[359] Bolstering the ideal that forward movement in the face of an uncertain outcome is worthwhile is a core tenet of hope that builds sustainable engagement around the possibility of improvement.[360] And while failure is a possibility, within deliberations, teachers should work to emphasize possibility rather than improbability and to develop that tendency within students.

Evaluation is the final stage in the inquiry model, signaling completion of one or more ends-in-view and the need for reflection and critique. Students compare their results to the defined markers of success. Emphasis should be placed on recognizing the knowledge gained through the solution attempt.[361] Evaluating outcomes provides useful information for moving forward, and future intelligent action is founded on such information. Evaluating outcomes goes beyond a simple dichotomy of success or failure. A more nuanced reflection allows for deeper understanding that is valuable for future problem-solving attempts. For example, if the desired changes have been achieved, but sustaining them requires ongoing attention, students must determine whether they can continue to commit to such ongoing activity to maintain the positive outcome. Or if the outcome did not fully match with the measures of success, but additional efforts seem capable of bringing about success, students may determine to add more time and effort into the project. If the outcome was deemed a failure, students need to engage with possible factors in that failure, considering whether a previously unidentified barrier blocked success but may now be overcome in light of the new understandings generated. If the failure seems related to the lack of full implementation or follow-through, students may resolve to reengage more fully or abandon the project as too costly. In the end, students receive new information as a result of their action, no matter the level of success. Moreover, developing such habits of hope changes the individual's identity, allowing each to see herself as possessing the potential to change their circumstances through focused action. Reflection not only enables us to restructure our worlds and our hopes but also can help us better understand our lives with others, our desires, and ourselves.[362]

The call to deliberation is especially important in light of the increased support for authoritarian rulers and the present climate of self-interest and distrust that is widespread in America. A noted champion of such deliberation, Amy Gutmann explains,

> The willingness to deliberate about mutually binding matters distinguishes democratic citizens from self-interested citizens, who argue merely to advance their own interests, and deferential citizens, who turn themselves into passive subjects by failing to argue, out of deference to political authority. Justice is far more likely to be served by democratic citizens who reason together in search of mutually justifiable decisions than it is by people who are uninterested in politics or interested in it only for the sake of power.[363]

The habit of using deliberation and its related habits of respectful listening, information seeking, and consensus building, are central to developing active, hopeful citizens who do not rely on or succumb to authoritarian leaders. We must take talking and listening, and the deliberation they contribute to, seriously in the development of good citizens who are capable of hoping together.

Foster Criticality and Dissent

Criticality taps into the reconstructive spirit of hope, identifying how our present life falls short of what we want, articulating the problem, and putting forward alternatives. Criticality can be carefully honed so that it does not become bogged down in complaining or lead one to throw in the towel, believing that improvement is impossible. Teachers can develop critical thinking with a spirit of criticality, where such thinking is not merely thinking deeply or rationally, but rather goes further to identify injustice, interrogate power structures, and assert practices of democracy that enable citizens to flourish. Such criticality works against the status quo toward greater understanding of the complex systems within which we operate and how to change them. In this regard, the critical aspect of hope distinguishes it from just grit or perseverance, which leaves injustice and problematic conditions in place. Critical analysis should extend to even our most enduring principles of democracy, questioning their continued role and viability, enabling students to affirm those principles for themselves or revise them if needed.

Similar to Generation Z's emphasis on fixing root causes of problems, hope moves from recognition of problems to critical analysis of their contributing factors and conditions to dissenting or transformative action in light of them. Within schools, students can be sensitized to aspects of injustice or problematic constraints on liberty so that they learn how to identify them. And students can be supported through questioning and challenging those constraints or injustice in order to see that such action is worthwhile and can have a positive impact on the world. Teachers can nurture students' dispositions to question and challenge, rather than to accept and obey. At the same time, they can talk with students about the importance and, at times, even responsibility one bears for addressing such constraint or injustice. Such conversations can help students see that criticality and dissent are not about mere rebel rousing or attention seeking, but instead engage democracy and, at times, civil disobedience, to maintain freedom, fairness, and order. In Dewey's words,

> A society which makes provision for participation in its good of all its members on equal terms and which secures flexible readjustment of its institutions through interaction of the different forms of associated life is in so far democratic. Such a society must have a type of education which gives individuals a personal interest in social relationships and control, and the habits of mind which secure social changes without introducing disorder. [364]

Unlike cynicism, which drives individuals and democratic institutions apart, informed dissent through formal and informal avenues brings people together in a commitment to improving life's conditions.

Critical thinking and dissent rely on strong language skills. They are part of the inquiry process, where observations are made, facts are gathered, and participants discuss their experiences. But being critical does not mean coming to a quick or harsh judgment; rather it means carefully considering the genealogy of our conditions and how various stakeholders are implicated in or affected by them. To be an effective critic and to use criticism to shape one's hopes, and therefore one's action in the world, one needs a good understanding of language. Teachers should help students see how language works to wield power, to bring unity or division, and to persuade others. These skills can be inculcated in an array of ways: learning how to craft and deliver arguments for positions pertinent to students' lives, being pushed to test those arguments in experience, or challenging them in debate with disagreeing classmates. Certainly, there are already curricular opportunities within many schools that develop a child's ability to detect and evaluate arguments made by others (such as seventh-grade Common Core State Standards English Language Arts Standard 7.RI.8) and a child's ability to make claims and follow logical reasoning (7.WHST.1).[365] Teachers might further tailor lessons aimed at fulfilling those standards and others like them to real-life examples from democracy within and outside school walls.

To craft objects and objectives of hope, students must develop skills of historical critique. This involves critiquing the events that have led to our current values and ways of life, including our current struggles with despair and disengagement. To do so, students must have a working knowledge of historical facts and events in order to make valid assessments about the good life they envision today and in the future. In other words, they have to know history to know how to answer, "What should I hope for?" And, helpfully, history also reveals evidence of meliorism, which can help bolster students' beliefs that their efforts are justified and capable of producing meaningful impact on the world.

To support students' capacities to envision a different, unfamiliar reality, teachers should tap into the rich accounts of impactful historic figures or grassroots movements. Importantly, students need access to stories that have not been sanitized to produce happy endings, but instead should include accounts of struggle and failure in decision-making. Allow students to witness the turmoil that figures such as Reverend Martin Luther King or Nelson Mandela endured, instead of viewing them from the successful ending perspectives of achieving greater civil rights or the abolishment of apartheid. Use biographies and personal accounts to help students see how those exemplars creatively generated possible solutions while wrestling with the potential negative impacts of their choices on themselves and their loved ones, and ultimately moved past bitter disappointments. These accounts provide significant insights into the real thoughts and doubts with which hopers engage, which may help students see them as real people similar to themselves rather than rarely exceptional. Students may later reflect and draw on those examples when facing their own obstacles, finding similarity in their struggles and perhaps solidarity and motivation as a result. One especially worthwhile example that may appeal to teens because it is written by teens is the account of the Parkland, Florida, students who led the March for our Lives.[366] In their book, they detail their incredible loss, their anger and surprise at the power of the gun lobby over legislators who seemed unwilling to truly hear their calls for counselors rather than armed teachers, their recognition of the difficulty of fulfilling their hopeful vision for safer schools, and their feelings of motivation to continue their work in the face of setbacks.

When reading such accounts, it is important for teachers to pause for students to consider how the historic person likely felt in that moment. Allow the student to imagine himself as a participant alongside the figure. For example, the National Underground Railroad Freedom Center in Cincinnati, Ohio, provides students with an immersive video experience that allows them to feel both the hope of escape and the fear of capture that a slave might have undergone. In the midst of such an experience, the teacher might hone a child's skills of imagination so that she envisions a detailed plan for escape and hope for a better life that was guided and constrained by the realities of the situation at the time.

To distinguish what is possible, feasible, and helpful from what is not, young citizens require knowledge of history, of what has been tried before, and scientific facts about what is realistic in our world. History provides resources for hope. Or, as Rebecca Solnit, social commentator on hope, says of hoping, "We have the past. Which gives us patterns, models, parallels, principles and resources, and stories of heroism, brilliance, persistence, and the deep joy to be found in doing the work that matters."[367] Students should learn about the trajectory of our democracy, including how its principles have supported its growth and have adapted over time. Learning about that trajectory can help students appreciate how democracy has supported hope and enhanced our lives. That historical chart exposes students to examples of how success and well-being have been contingent on others. In other words, they are exposed to the social and political elements of how hope has played out across time.

Teachers should hone students' abilities to ask tough questions that reveal how power works in social situations, including how it privileges some people and not others. Teachers might also take students to protests and other events where groups are putting forward critiques as part of their vision of hope. At the very least, they could engage students in analyzing what protestors are doing well and what they are not, and whether they are improving democratic living, even from a distance or back in the classroom. Although protests may appear new or spontaneous, teachers can reveal their lengthy histories of activism and organizing so that students have a sense of the persistence and struggle often long at work in protests. Teachers can generate new stories about the importance of protests, showing how they are useful places to engage in and pursue objects of hope. Thereby, teachers may prevent or work against fatalistic views of protests as being an ineffective waste of time or views of protests as being merely the work of paid actors or the sort of chaos that should be squelched by authoritarian leaders. And, when appropriate, teachers could channel students' own frustrations with the current state of affairs as they discuss their hopes for the future by engaging the students in acts of critique and dissent.

Student walkouts following the shootings in Parkland, Florida, are one educative example. Those walkouts resulted from students feeling unsafe in their schools and are aligned with creating visions and bringing about practices that are safer and more welcoming in their schools. The walkouts have demonstrated success for students in several ways: attracting media attention to showcase the problem, starting conversations with elected officials on gun policy reform, prompting new policies on school violence, and helping students to experience a sense of agency and empowerment that may lead to further political and civil participation. The walkouts have also shifted some public impressions of youth as being spoiled or apathetic, revealing their deep concerns and experiences with the legitimate social problem of gun violence. Teachers, however, must help students see that protest is an early step, not a terminus. Students need further support as they move toward sustainable and significant changes in school culture, safety, and legislation. Moreover, teachers should highlight the attention received by the Parkland protestors to reveal the significance of whose stories about struggle, injustice, and reform are featured or heard and where those tellers are located economically and sociopolitically. For example, well before the

Parkland walkouts of largely white suburban students, many urban poor students of color were leading protests regarding gun violence in their communities, yet their stories largely went unheard. Students must be attuned to such differences and what they reveal about power imbalances in our country today as they envision a better future and as they build coalitions that should acknowledge earlier efforts and differing experiences and aspects of similar problems.

Finally, teachers can employ approaches designed to facilitate hope and citizenship development. Some examples of extracurricular programs and school-based curricula include *Discovering Justice, iCivics, Public Achievement, Freechild, Street Law*, or *Mikva Challenge*. These programs help students learn about US laws and values as well as how to critique them, research community issues, get involved politically, use their agency to solve social problems together, analyze power, and to take a stand when fighting for one's own well-being as well as that of others. They enable children to learn *through* democracy and enacting citizenship in the present, rather than just *about* democracy and their future citizenship post-graduation.

Cultivate Imagination and Storytelling

Imagination and storytelling are important to hoping because they help us envision the better world we desire and rally others around that vision. Imagination has past, present, and future aspects. Imagination involves looking at the present from the perspective of what may be possible. But when it comes to pragmatist hope, this is not unchecked possibility, but rather insofar as pragmatism urges keeping one's feet planted in reality, imagination must account for our embodied experience of the natural world and for the structural limitations that linger from history. Imagination is not the radical creation of something entirely new, but rather an envisioning of what might grow out of what is and what has been. It also helps us to better grasp the present, for "imagination gives us a critical distance to the present that allows us to draw connections and to understand our world."[368] Finally, it helps to provide focus and structure as we move forward into the future.

Imagination happens while conducting inquiry, as we try to understand a situation by considering what is actual and what might be possible as a result of our hypotheses and action. It works ahead to anticipate what might unfold. Dewey explains, "the trial is in imagination, not in overt fact. The experiment is carried on by tentative rehearsals in thought which do not affect physical facts outside the body. Thought runs ahead and foresees outcomes, and thereby avoids having to wait the instruction of actual failure or disaster."[369] Imagination helps us combine means and ends so that we can find our way out of problematic situations. It helps us envision alternatives and chart new directions. Imagination can generate possibilities and the conditions that activate them. Imagination gives us ideas and directions for how to enact hope.

Inquiry into the impact of a problem and potential solutions includes obtaining the perspectives of others. Obviously, firsthand accounts are highly valuable here; but imagination can also play a rather significant role. Imagination can include consideration of how people different from oneself experience a problem or the world around them, such as white people imagining the plight of people of color. Such imagination can build empathy, a desire to connect across differences, and a moral drive to work to alleviate further suffering of others. Imagination can be a motivator to overcome the distancing related to despair and cynicism, to engage habits of hope toward improving our world on behalf of those different from ourselves.

When some groups have had little interaction with others or hold false stereotypes about them, imagination might exacerbate problems. A concern is that individuals might envision the lives of those different from themselves in harmfully faulty ways, such as white people imagining black people as inferior or unintelligent. I follow Christopher LeBron in responding to that potential problem by holding that

> the erroneous holding of racial beliefs is not imagination gone wrong— rather, it is the result of one having not used any imagination at all. The very dangerous thing about ideology is that one accepts without much reflection heuristic interpretive shortcuts to make systematic sense of the world, and quite frequently, these shortcuts are generated by power holders and accepted by those who benefit from acquiescing. Imagination, by contrast . . . leads to possibly revolutionary ideas.[370]

Imagination entails the sort of hard work and critical reflection that can push past those accepted and problematic ideologies to work toward new understandings across difference. Imagination does not generate ideas from nothing, but rather from our experiences of the world. It includes being welcoming to hearing the life stories provided by those different from us and being receptive to the experiences contained therein as a starting point for imagining how others have lived in the past and present and how they might life in the future. Notably, those stories often serve as a check on stereotypes if we listen carefully to them. Being receptive is a proclivity toward accepting those alternatives as a source for future thinking and effort. An education in imagination partly entails learning how to break from routine ways of seeing others so that we can envision others and ourselves differently.

Storytelling is one of the primary ways that we engage extended imagination and convey our vision of the future, thereby building culture and identity. Stories can help us out of ruts because they give us accounts of how problems can be solved and how life can be better—a check on the apathy increasingly prevalent today. Stories can move us from passivity to participation, showing us both examples of how to take action and why it's worthwhile to do so. All the while, stories depict the objects and objectives of hope; they give us ways to express the better future we desire, as well as who we are and what it means to be an American.

Our stories often depict how the world is and how it could be. And those stories can serve as a rallying point for others, articulating and bringing us together around shared objects or objectives of hope. While the World Values Survey may reveal some worrisome things about the state of democracy today, it also demonstrates that "mass self-expression values are extremely important in the emergence and flourishing of democratic institutions in a society."[371] Telling stories about ourselves and the world we desire is an important way of being heard and of feeling valued in a democracy. Constructing narratives of our shared hopes arising from our collective history and struggles, yet leaving them open ended and revisable so that citizens can contribute to them and change them as conditions unfold is one way that we write the story of democracy. Importantly, those narratives must acknowledge and face the atrocities of injustice in our American past and present even as we construct our hopes for the future. It is especially important that Americans who have been denied opportunities to hope or significantly improve their lives in the past because of laws and practices enforced by fellow citizens have those experiences validated, and that amends are made where possible.

We need to spend more time accounting for trauma and harm in our lives and in the stories we tell. In rushing past them, we risk an array of problems, not the least of which is reinforcing a progress narrative or celebrating improvement over time when we need to be sitting with suffering to process it, assign/take responsibility for it, and work through it. For example, teachers might engage students in analyzing, comparing, and contrasting the struggles, fear, suffering, and power dynamics evident within the Storytellers Project. While the project is a collection of stories from across the country intended to "celebrate our country's diversity through the stories that bind us together," we must also pause to consider how those connections are forged in light of past and lingering suffering.[372]

Within schools, teachers may guide the important work of imagination and storytelling. Creative writing and language arts courses can cultivate students' self-expression so that they learn how to put forward their experience of the world, to lay claim to it, and to integrate themselves into a community of stakeholders. It's important that we learn how to tell our own stories individually, but collective storytelling often offers even more important rewards. Working alongside others to understand their interpretation of an event can help to forge collective truths about current life that account for multiple perspectives in a pragmatist spirit. It requires careful listening to one another and attention to the details, emotions, and experiences that have shaped various events. To come to empathize with others, when appropriate, we must first listen in ways that extend us beyond our own belief systems or slow our rush to judgment. Through collective storytelling, storytellers engage in complex social action to take a collaborative approach to envisioning the best resolution of a situation for all parties. Finally, this practice builds coalitions that can draw on each other's strengths and achieve mutual empowerment. Altogether, these aspects of collective storytelling embody practices of critical social thought and deliberation guided by empathy and geared toward coordinated social action.

Stories can be used to show students how their worlds could be different. Stories of struggle and success can be used to develop sensitivity to the lives of other people, to encounter emotional struggles, and to provide examples of creative solutions to real problems. When students see how others have worked to improve their lives, they are provided fodder for how they might try out ideas in their own situations. Stories provide an arsenal of examples to be employed, wielded, and tested while providing counterevidence to fatalistic claims that "there's nothing that can be done" or "it's not worth the effort." Stories help to generate and engage possibilities.

Narrative texts whose protagonists must wrestle with problems can be used to generate discussion around those problems. Students are able to witness the character's inner struggle through a transparent process. *The Giver* by Lois Lowry provides an example of a character who discovers a significant, hidden problem and chooses to act to improve the situation.[373] Jonas, assigned to become the new Receiver, discovers that the seemingly utopian world in which he lives euthanizes individuals regularly, and that his foster brother, Gabe, is scheduled for this fate. Jonas moves toward hope by creating a well-conceived plan with a full awareness of the cost of failure. Thus, biographical accounts and literature build habits of hope in students by offering a means to consider problematic situations in light of fear and possibility. [374]

Teachers can employ stories in ways that cultivate habits of hope. Stories are most effective at doing so when they are meaningful to students, often because the students relate to the real, problematic situations described in the stories. By detecting similarities and seeing themselves in the stories, students may be ushered into self-reflection. Teachers can help to facilitate that self-reflection by engaging students in discussions and assignments that pull students' habits into view and provoke reexamination of them if warranted. Finally, teachers can use stories and self-reflective exercises to help students appreciate their own past agency and achievement to bolster confidence at and proclivity toward continued effort.

Teachers can also engage students in interpreting and critiquing legislators' visions for the future, put forward through their policy proposals and campaign trail anecdotes. Students can explore their feasibility and desirability, all the while seeking what their role might be in those stories, if anything at all. This helps young citizens determine which legislators are worthy of their support, enabling them to make informed preferences or voting decisions based on shared hopes for the future. In each of these examples, imagination and storytelling enable students to better understand themselves, identify their envisioned America, and build identity with others based on that vision.

Finally, storytelling should not be understood as only written or oral; it is also visual and public. Artists Alice Rose George and Lee Marks tapped into this with their collection, *Hope Photographs*.[375] These images depict hope through significant feats of collective work, such as a rocket blasting into the sky and Buzz Aldrin walking on the moon, and through moments of individual effort as simple as an AIDS patient raising his hand toward a lighted window to greet the new day, and as courageous as a political protestor facing down the tanks in Tiananmen Square. One related example, the Hope Camera Project, highlights storytelling that engages visual representations of hope woven together with narratives and then shared with the public. This project for fourth and fifth graders was undertaken by

Jennifer Magnuson-Stessman, a school counselor. She asked the students to take twenty-eight photos during the week of things that made them feel hopeful. They turned to both significant and seemingly mundane aspects of their lives to visually depict such hope. Then, they wrote an essay to tell their story of hope represented by the images. Finally, the photos and stories were publicly displayed at an art show where the students talked with guests about their stories and depictions of hope, thereby serving as fodder for the development of shared hopes and seeing connections with others.

View Citizenship as Shared Fate

In times of national struggle, America has often sought unification through patriotism. For example, Americans joined together in the days immediately following September 11, 2001. We united under images of strength and history, such as displaying our flag and through shared practices, like singing patriotic tunes on the steps of the Capitol. Patriotism positively entails pride in who we are as a country, and a sense of commitment to seeing our country through into the future. Patriotism should not be blind, unreflective, or permanent allegiance; rather, it should be informed commitment with full recognition of the areas in which our country needs improvement. Indeed, many patriots work to ameliorate those areas. Importantly, patriotism should not be confused with nationalism, wherein our country is seen as unquestioningly superior to others and where we put our interests above all others'. Patriotism, however, should invite conversation about what America is and how it can be better.

As we create a new story that unites and moves us forward in hope, we must beware of the potential pitfalls of nationalism, while still celebrating patriotic pride in our country and its possibilities. One way we can achieve this is through viewing citizenship as shared fate, where, despite acknowledging our significant differences, we foreground the ways we are linked together by location, history, culture, and more. Citizenship as shared fate urges us to interpret our experiences and events in America through how they mutually impact us as members of the larger American community. Sharing a fate differs from just having a common fate; it entails a more active role in shaping that future and preserving the well-being of America within it.[376] That future doesn't just happen to all of us simultaneously. Developing citizenship as shared fate nurtures the relational aspects of citizenship. It builds the inclination to care for others across that community, even though they may differ significantly from us, because we recognize the many ways in which our futures are bound together politically, geographically, economically, and culturally, and that they can be improved by cooperating together. That inclination, one aligned with a sense of responsibility for the well-being of others that can be supported by teachers, leads us to consider the effects of our political choices on others and work toward the best interests of the group.

Citizenship as shared fate can still provide a sense of "us," and pride in that identity, but, unlike nationalism, it is an affinity that is more readily reconsidered and open to change based on shifting circumstances and social ties that we choose to emphasize. Moreover, that identity is one we construct through our relations to others and by shaping our nation. Citizenship as shared fate is an inclination to interpret events in terms of their impact on the "us" that composes a public of authentically connected people rather than a formal collection dictated by citizenship as only a geographical status. We are brought together to interpret and negotiate what it means to be a citizen, which is significant in our environment, where the demographics of our population are changing. Moreover, citizenship as shared fate raises a bigger tent, more inclusively bringing people into the "us." It unites people in a political climate that too often casts people in an "us versus them." For example, while a long-standing narrative of cowboys versus Indians pervades American pop culture and even history textbooks, these two groups united in response to the Keystone XL pipeline, recognizing worrisome implications for their shared fate in light of the pipeline's construction.[377] Foregrounding mutual stake in social problems is a useful way to span diverse or otherwise conflicting groups.

Our larger world is also changing, forcing new considerations of national identity as technology, communication, and the economy have drawn people from around the world together in new ways. Even when they may live far apart, citizenship as shared fate helps to build bridges of concern between people. It causes citizens to think about and act in the interest of those in their local communities, and also to consider how their actions impact those across the country and even abroad. At the same time, it recognizes that the shared history, values, struggles, and successes of our country continue to shape our fate today and those of our neighbors elsewhere. Citizenship as shared fate gives rise to a new form of patriotism as relation and connection to one's countrymen, location, and past.

Attending to shared fate requires an initial grounding in care for the future. Teachers need to work to invest students in the future—to help them to see why it matters for their lives and others, and to see how they can play a role in shaping it. Students need to see themselves as not only in the future but also of value to that future. This builds not only self-care, but also a sense of care about others who will inhabit that future with them. Hal Hershfield, a researcher at New York University has shown that "people who are primed to be aware of their future self . . . focus more on their best interest and/or the best interest of society, compared with participants who haven't made the connection between now and the future."[378] Being invested in the future can help to curb suicide and so-called despair deaths insofar as it helps individuals project a valuable life worth living for themselves. Developing investment in the future can also help to address the population of Americans who believe the past was better and are less satisfied with democracy today. It can provide them avenues to enliven some valued aspects of American life that have dwindled and perhaps help them reaffirm their commitment to democracy, as they recognize that not only is time marching on but also they can have a role to play in shaping influences on themselves and others.

Teachers can engage shared fate by involving students in projects that explore the impact of an issue on a community. For example, as trade wars and large-scale milk and meat contracts threaten the stability of family farms, some rural families are considering fracking as a way to provide additional income to keep those farms operable and rural communities viable. While ultimately deciding whether or not to participate may be up to each individual landowner, teachers in those areas could guide students through a reflection on the potential economic, cultural, environmental, and other consequences of deciding to engage in fracking on family farmland. Teachers could help students in rural classrooms see how their families, classmates, and neighbors might be impacted, as well as how the power grid and energy corporations might also be affected. Teachers can also help students figure out if their personal aims are aligned or in conflict with the aims and needs of other people. Teachers could bring civil society organizations and public agencies, such as the Farm Bureau and Cooperative Extension, into the classroom to better understand the ramifications of potential decisions. And school-based organizations like the Future Farmers of America might provide additional resources and space for deeper discussion of implications on youth outside of, but connected to, the primary classroom. This form of teaching directly engages democracy, as students seek to understand a shared problem, solve it with others, and protect the future of their community as they do so. It also helps students to see that they are "interdependent, folded up in their shared ends" and that their loyalty to the community and collaboration within it is warranted because of their shared long-term interests.[379]

Service learning is another way to foster shared fate, as it brings together "community service and academic study of the issue being addressed by the students' service."[380] Within service learning, students learn how to identify social problems, respond out of a sense of shared responsibility, act to help those in need, work to transform the situation, and then engage in guided reflection about their experiences. Service learning gives students first-hand interactions with others who are struggling with an issue. Students often need to have those delicate and difficult interactions facilitated by a skilled teacher. Such a teacher can also guide students in seeing points of connection between themselves and other people, whether through similar experiences and emotions or through facing similar outcomes. When one is unable to see shared aspects of humanity, one may not care for the well-being of others; teaching for shared fate works against that tendency. Service learning projects can help students craft reasonable ends-in-view that acknowledge the limitations of the present world while still trying to improve on it. Even small and piecemeal successes can help bolster students' agency by affirming their ability to make a difference and showing that their effort is worthwhile.

Service learning and related pedagogical techniques that intimately join students with others are especially important given our current context of disconnect, our focus on individual success, and our history of ignoring segments of our society plagued by hardship and struggle—places and communities that may seem unsafe or undesirable to connect to our classrooms. Glaude reminds us that we should

envision the beloved community in which *all* Americans do more than just go to work and tend to their individual gardens, but experience a deeply felt interdependence in a jointly shared effort to reimagine American democracy. Americans have to live together, in the deepest sense of the phrase—to make a life together that affords everyone (and I mean everyone) a real chance. This can happen only when we experience genuine connectedness, when the well-being of African Americans is bound up with any consideration of the well-being of the nation.[381]

Teachers and schools should enable experiences that connect students with others in authentic ways, encourage students to reflect on the significance of such connections, and consider how they reshape citizenship as shared fate. This includes making race and other aspects of difference explicitly foregrounded within our considerations of shared fate, rather than ignoring it or making it an afterthought.

While we know that service learning approaches are effective ways to prepare good citizens, they are quite rare in our classrooms.[382] Some of the best models for such education come from programs like Generation Citizen.[383] Teaching how to hope may mean sizable shifts in the content and approach of typical citizenship education, putting real-life engagement with social problems in local communities, connectedness to others, and service learning at the forefront of classroom practice.

Build Trust

Right now, lack of trust is one of the biggest roadblocks to hope in America. Collective effort toward objects and objectives of hope requires not only that people be able to collaborate with other another but also that they be able to depend on each other for assistance and generally believe that the judgments and motivations of others are wise and just. Sometimes, lack of trust is warranted and beneficial. Some level of distrust is built into the American democratic system of checks and balances, where we rely on our institutions, branches of government, and elected leaders to hold a degree of skepticism toward each other. Between individuals, trust typically functions as a horizontal relationship, yet many of our personal relationships are not fully horizontal, rather they are vertically structured by power and inequity, placing one person over another. Importantly, current lack of trust is justified in many ways and for many people, especially minorities who have been taken advantage of by those with greater power. And, in some cases, there is even warranted distrust among those with more power toward those with less power who may seek to even the score.[384] Making these relationships more horizontal is important to opening the way for trust and it may first require reconciliation for past harm.

But, distrust is growing in worrisome ways as our polarized citizenry becomes cordoned off from opposing views and makes ad hominem, and often stereotypical, attacks on the personal traits of those who hold opposing views. If we are to revive democracy and teach citizens how to hope, schools, other public institutions, and civil society organizations must affirm justified forms of distrust while primarily working to build trust. This endeavor relates to helping citizens see their shared fate and witness the effectiveness of coming together in community efforts to improve their own conditions and those of others.

Teachers may work to develop and assess trust, while verifying the worthwhileness of that trust, and scaffolding the hoping of students and their sense of self as capable agents.[385] Teachers who can demonstrate the impact of a student's effort to that student and others are more likely to produce future citizens who recognize their own agency and engage in civic action, rather than feeling ineffective and disengaging from democratic life, as we often see in America today.[386] Relatedly, we build trust by engaging in mutually supportive activities together, supporting the agency of others, and making ourselves vulnerable through recognition of our own need for support. When we learn to trust a peer—including his judgments and abilities—we scaffold him in developing his own agency. All the while, we may come to better care for that peer and his well-being. Then, the relationship we form with that peer may create a cycle of willingness to extend our trust out of concern for the relationship.[387]

When engaging in the collective work of hoping together, we build trust, in part, by making compromises. That means that we have to bend and give relative to each other in order to achieve mutual benefits. Too often today compromising is seen as a sign of weakness or surrender. Teachers can respond by sharing historical examples that reveal positive outcomes from compromising. They can also showcase the opposite, instances where unwillingness to compromise breeds stagnation and inability to address problems well or efficiently. At the same time, teachers can describe times when one may feel the need to stand one's ground and discuss criteria for differentiating that situation from those of more bull-headed stagnation. Recognizing that all is not lost when we compromise, that we can still maintain important elements of ourselves and our values when we compromise and yet can achieve significant overall outcomes, can help reveal reasons for trusting others. Emphasizing our shared fate within discussions and collective actions requiring compromise can provide an important reminder that we are "in this together" and that our shared future is better ensured when we work together rather than compete or draw a firm line in the sand between us.

Distrust sometimes arises from suspicion of someone else's intentions. Teachers can talk with students about the importance of clarifying motives and interests when working with others to solve problems, and encourage students to provide reasons for why they care about an issue or feel motivated to work to improve it. They should also discuss how their vision of the future impacts themselves and others. I am not so naive as to believe that all people will clearly share their true intentions, but when we start young, encouraging children to be truthful and forthright, we can work to establish an environment where we move toward greater transparency and justice. We can also talk overtly in schools about the value of aligning one's interests with the interests of others. That said, I also recognize that our country is increasingly swept up a spirit of individualism and in neoliberal economic and political pressures to look out for oneself and to compete against others to ensure one's own interests. These trends work against trust and collective effort, and are difficult to reverse. As a start, we must name the constraints of that environment and reveal its harm and limitations in order to call it into question.

Finally, my own position as someone who has largely lived a life of privilege and has not been significantly burned by others, may lead me to have greater faith in extending trust, which may appear naive to those who have been victims of abuse at the hands of others. Teachers, especially when working with historically marginalized and oppressed populations, must be especially sensitive to that history of harm and should help students develop an informed trust, so they are not easily taken advantage of, while also nurturing a guarded willingness to work with those who may have harmed them in the past. Teachers can equip students with skills for detecting and reducing the risks of trust, while also helping them see that trust can generate the conditions for collective action and improved living conditions. Improving conditions for trust requires first carefully attending to what has caused distrust in the first place, which in many cases includes white supremacy and racism. These must be overtly discussed and analyzed in classrooms so that students understand their lasting impact as well as ways to work against them. Building trust may also require restorative justice techniques that entail dominant individuals and groups recognizing and, when appropriate, taking responsibility for past harms perpetrated by themselves or those like them. Part of such work likely necessitates bringing different types of people together through civil organizations, social arrangements, and classroom experiences, where they can come to interact, learn from each other, discover shared humanity, and lay other foundational elements of trust. Teachers can encourage students to see goodness and possibility in others rather than as-suming mal intent. Ultimately, teachers can support students in having the courage to extend trust to others.

Going beyond Schools

Though I've focused on schools and citizenship education in particular, cul-tivating hope shouldn't be confined to schools. Children should learn how to hope in their homes, neighborhoods, sports teams, and clubs, not just within the classroom. And they should learn how to hope, not only from teachers but also from parents, friends, religious leaders, and more. Actually engaging in authentic democratic contexts and with civil society can go far beyond simply talking about or practicing related skills in the single, small setting of one classroom.[388] We should support an array of settings where hope is fos-tered, including in spaces that are significant to children, such as neighbor-hood festivals, youth poetry slams, and community gardens.[389] Importantly, much of the civic knowledge and identity of African American children, in particular, already takes place outside of schools within communities and churches, and across familial generations. While it is critical to expand school-based opportunities for citizenship education to these children, we should also support and magnify the useful work already occurring outside of school walls.[390]

Children are not the only people who can learn how to hope. Many of the educational practices outlined here can be extended into adult settings, whether they are formal learning environments or informal civil spaces. We might especially encourage the latter, supporting the expansion of civil so-ciety by recommending that our friends join clubs and organizations related to their areas of interest. Civil society is the primary space where publics form and act in a "sphere of social interaction" between large government life, private markets, and local family life.[391] Often civil society bridges these elements, interconnecting them and weaving together the individual with the community, freedoms, and regulations. Sometimes this involves com-promising or mediating conflicts between the practices and ideologies of the home, the economy, and the state through open communication among indi-viduals who come together in voluntary associations. They work together to expose tensions, and then seek to alleviate those tensions, or at least deter-mine how to live harmoniously in the midst of them.

As groups in civil society navigate the continuum from private to public, they encounter shifts in trust and power. They must transition from interacting with those with whom they share close bonds or common interests, to interacting with unfamiliar people and impersonalized arms of the government that wield significant power.[392] Civil society forms open associations and coalitions that engage together in communication, social movements, and other avenues to shape their surroundings, which ultimately influence the state and economy. Within such a space, citizens can self-mobilize to form relationships, communities, and publics that are not as restrictive and demanding as the family sphere (where blood ties often force action or interaction) because they are open and genuine. Civil society "is participatory and communal (like the public sector) yet voluntary and uncoercive (like the private sector)."[393] Civil society's voluntary nature offers an important space without undue state coercion for citizens to deliberate about laws, institutions, and practices of democracy to determine whether they are just or legitimate. It provides citizens a space to share and compare their assessments, as well as to openly proclaim their consent in public ways, thereby strengthening democracy and affirming its alignment with citizens' beliefs, needs, and desires.[394]

Let's consider one example. Early in 2019 a group of Democratic lawmakers proposed a set of programs to address climate change dubbed the "Green New Deal." One aspect of these proposals dealt with limiting the carbon footprint and emissions of farms. Ranchers and farmers from across the country, most of whom identify as Republicans, perceived that their livelihoods were misunderstood by Democrats in cities far away, at best, and that their very way of life was on the verge of being extinguished by unjustified, uninformed, or unreasonable regulations, at worst. Many of these citizens belong to the Farm Bureau, a nationwide civil organization with state and local branches. Sensing a threat and trying to make sense of the problem of climate change and potential solutions posed by others, farmers and ranchers formed small publics. In their local chapters, they took to discussing the issue, deliberating about the proposed Green New Deal. From those deliberations, some members then turned outward to publicly share their unique perspectives as family farmers whose futures are on the line in light of potential new regulations and to demonstrate environmental efforts already undertaken by many farmers who see themselves as stewards of the earth.[395] Some state leaders used media outlets to speak out.[396] Now many Farm Bureau members are working to sort out solutions that enable their livelihoods to continue while also furthering efforts to protect the environment. In these ways, the Farm Bureau is enabling citizens to deliberate about legislation, present their alternative views, and affirm their needs, thereby facilitating democratic practices and political impact.

Within civil society, citizens can acquire tools to support themselves when they are struggling and a network of people with whom they can hope together. They may experience solidarity with others around issues of shared concern, which helps to build trust, identity, and agency. Moreover, in a setting where many citizens feel left behind, as though their concerns have not been fully acknowledged or attended to by their leaders, civil outlets may help them feel heard and nurture their own agency instead of hostility.

Community organizations often involve volunteer work, which, when aligned with the method of inquiry and reflection, can be one way in which citizens are introduced to hoping and discover firsthand the impact of shared work. Being active in civil life helps one to become a part of society, thereby fighting against current trends of apathy and disengagement. Additionally, learning how to use power through voting, formal institutions, and movement building that make up political life can provide the tools to leverage change to meet a group's needs and fulfill the objects of hope that they set. We know, though, that in our efforts to rethink and improve civil society,

> Most people need to be directly invited into public engagements, contacted personally by leaders and folks they know. People must also "see themselves" in the shared undertaking. And they must believe an undertaking will really matter—or else they won't bother. All of these considerations direct our attention to the changing roles of leaders, to shifting social identities and modes of organization, and to considerations of power, resources, and institutional leverage.[397]

As educators and concerned citizens, we must offer these invitations and extend supportive conditions to others. As participation in civil organizations dwindles and becomes increasingly segregated, citizens seeking to resuscitate democracy must perhaps first breathe new energy into these spaces.

Finally, adults can use technology (an important but limited resource within so-called civic deserts) to broaden their interactions with others, widening their sources of information and opportunities to exchange and deliberate, so that they can extend their concerns for shared fate to circles outside of just their civil organizations or segregated communities. Scattered and fledgling publics can use technology to learn from each other, to share stories of success, and to bolster one another's efforts. Such outreach is also an important part of making sure that inquiry is well informed and that our visions of hope bring about flourishing lives rather than harm to others. Connecting with individuals and groups outside of one's primary networks may work against today's trend toward self-interestedness and echo chambers. Even as many traditional civil society organizations are declining or increasingly segregated, technology may open new doors for affiliation and expansion.

Technology can also be harnessed to enable the development and sharing of stories, including accounts of past experiences in America and depictions of what America might become. Storytelling classes can develop skills of expression, description, and persuasion. Storytelling contests can encourage citizens to imagine new and better worlds, while also providing a platform to share stories that can be validated by others as we continue to define what it means to be American.[398] These stories can change what Charles Taylor calls the social imaginary—the expectations we have of each other and what is reasonable to expect from each other. Changing the social imaginary can build trust and support the practice of hoping together. The impact of stories, especially when shared widely via technology, can have wide-ranging impact on who we are and how we understand ourselves. It can even shape formal elements of democracy, perhaps leading to hope-based legislation like the GI Bill, which sought to improve the common good and bring about greater equity for citizens. It informed a vision of a better life for America and its individual citizens, aided by their own agency in achieving it. It told a story of patriotism, participation, education, and effort in America.

A Call to Hope

In sum, learning how to hope is much more than just teaching good citizenship and is certainly more than developing grit. Teaching hope cultivates habits, nurturing proclivities to undertake effort to improve one's life and the lives of others. Those habits must be situated within a larger practice of educating for democracy. They are supported by learning within communities of inquiry that deliberate about and experiment with best courses of action, with shared fate guiding their decisions. Those classrooms should be oriented around the question "What should we do?," a question that engages the pragmatist spirit of hope as collective engagement toward possibility and action.[399] When those courses of action include actively participating in formal and informal aspects of democracy—from contacting elected policymakers to holding a community conversation about an issue—our young citizens develop not only skills but also confidence and proclivities that increase their likelihood of future participation, thereby countering recent trends of disengagement. Learning skills of criticality and dissent, becoming imaginative storytellers, and developing robust understanding of history and democracy provides students know-how in shaping their objects and objectives of hope, as well as their practices of hoping together. Schools that engage in this sort of active, issues-based citizenship education not only teach how to hope but also showcase for students and the broader community that democracy is more vibrant when we hope.

While immensely important, this call to teach hope is also immensely challenging. Learning how to hope is likely most effective when teachers demonstrate and model hoping and when classrooms are part of communities that engage in and support hoping. Yet, teachers already feel overburdened with a wide array of expectations—from teaching subject matter to being disciplinarians and from providing mentorship to ensuring students' basic needs are met. Teachers may also feel unprepared to teach hope when they themselves may feel lost in despair or are cynical about our political system or when they are overwhelmed by violence and injustice witnessed in their schools. And they may struggle to hope when they work in settings where they feel professionally undervalued and have dwindling resources. Finally, the approach to teaching citizens how to hope also faces substantial obstacles, such as the risks and kickback of exploring controversial political and social issues in the classroom.[400] To support the hope of teachers, we must value their knowledge, experience, and pedagogical choices, reflecting it in the policies and practices we endorse. Teachers also need to be able to employ their own agency in changing and shaping their circumstances in schools. And teachers need administrators and families who support them, including when they venture into politically controversial waters with the topics they select for their classroom. Each of these helps to enable teachers to engage in hoping and thereby model hoping for children. Although the task of reviving democracy through teaching citizens how to hope is a monumental one, it may be one of teachers' most important contributions to our country.

Even though I've focused most on teaching students how to hope, this book is a call to hope across our citizenry. While starting with children who are malleable may help to head off some antidemocratic tendencies in adulthood, many of our older citizens must also develop new proclivities if we are to maintain and improve democracy as a form of government and as a way of life. The school-based practices advocated here can be used or adapted for college campuses and adults outside of schools to grow their habits of hope.

I opened this book by asking several questions and I return to them now. These questions are especially important as our country struggles with despair and cynicism, as citizens increasingly disengage in political participation and turn to authoritarian leaders, and as we move into new election seasons wondering what lies ahead. "Are there reasons to hope?" Yes, we are those very reasons. We have the ability to create, engage, and sustain hope through our habits. And we can turn to civil society and schools to provide an answer to "How can I hope?" There, we can nurture our skills of inquiry, imagination, and agency so that we become skilled and persistent hopers who both support and are supported by democracy. That sort of hope is deeper, more sustainable, and more actionable that the hope typically championed in campaign slogans or in today's common accounts of privatized hope for one's own self-interests.

Understanding and seeking out such pragmatist hope may also help us identify leaders during elections who will better support our efforts as citizens, regardless of political party. Those are leaders who listen to and learn from our visions of the future as they construct stories of what America might become. And they are leaders who build trust and encourage collaborative efforts to solve social problems. They are leaders that support education, appreciate scientific exploration, and encourage communities of inquiry, valuing the new ideas that each brings. They are leaders that facilitate our hoping, rather than leaders we merely place hope in.

Finally, within our communities and through the stories we construct about our American identity, our prospects, and the principles that we uphold, we can answer, "What should I hope for?" We are the interpreters of our past and the authors of our future. Hoping shapes how democracy is understood, whether it is valued, and what many of its principles and aims are. Let us learn how to hope so that we can revive democracy.

Notes

Chapter 1

1. John Dewey, "The Challenge of Democracy to Education," in *John Dewey: The Later Works, 1925–1953*, vol. 11: 181–201.
2. "Suicide Rising across the US," Centers for Disease Control and Prevention, last modified June 11, 2018, https://www.cdc.gov/vitalsigns/suicide/index.html; Tara Haelle, "Hospitals See Growing Numbers of Kids and Teens at Risk for Suicide," *National Public Radio*, May 16, 2018, https://www.npr.org/sections/health-shots/2018/05/16/611407972/hospitals-see-growing-numbers-of-kids-and-teens-at-risk-for-suicide.
3. In the final clause here, I do not mean to suggest an imperialist sense of taking action on behalf of others, but rather a sense of collective action often done in solidarity with those others.
4. Walt Whitman, "Democratic Vistas," in *Prose Works 1892: The Collected Writings of Walt Whitman Volume II*, edited by Floyd Stovall (New York: New York University Press, 1964), 393.
5. Yascha Mounk, *The People vs Democracy: Why Our Freedom Is in Danger and How to Save It* (Cambridge, MA: Harvard University Press, 2018), 18.
6. "Address at a Luncheon Meeting of the National Industrial Conference Board (33)," February 13, 1961, Public Papers of the Presidents: John F. Kennedy, 1961.
7. William J. Clinton, "Address Accepting the Presidential Nomination at the Democratic National Convention in New York—July 16, 1992," The American Presidency Project, accessed May 22, 2018, http://www.presidency.ucsb.edu/ws/?pid=25958.
8. Barack H. Obama, "Acceptance Speech at Democratic National Convention," Denver, August 28, 2008.
9. Barack H. Obama, *The Audacity of Hope* (New York: Random House, 2006), 11.
10. Barack H. Obama, "Remarks by the President on Election Night," National Archives and Records Administration, November 7, 2012, https://obamawhitehouse.archives.gov/the-press-office/2012/11/07/remarks-president-election-night.
11. Ibid.
12. Ronald W. Reagan, "Farewell Address to the Nation—January 11, 1989," The American Presidency Project, accessed May 22, 2018, http://www.presidency.ucsb.edu/ws/?pid=29650.
13. George H. W. Bush, "Address Accepting the Presidential Nomination at the Republican National Convention—August 18, 1988," The American Presidency Project, accessed May 22, 2018, http://www.presidency.ucsb.edu/ws/index.php?pid=25955.
14. James T. Kloppenberg, "Trump's Inaugural Address Was a Radical Break with American Tradition," *Washington Post*, January 20, 2017.

15. Chloe Lemmel-Hay, "Let America Hope Again," *Harvard Political Review*, January 27, 2017, http://harvardpolitics.com/culture/let-america-hope-again/.

16. Roberto Stefan Foa and Yascha Mounk, "The Danger of Deconsolidation: The Democratic Disconnect," *Journal of Democracy*, 27 (2016): 5–17, 7. I want to be careful not to overstate the perilous position of our democracy, which some critics allege Foa and Mounk have done. Instead, I want to look more carefully at how some of the aspects of political life they highlight can be used to consider despair and teach hope.

17. Admittedly, while some of this withdrawal is intentional, other forms of withdrawal are less conscious, and still others are at the hands of those who exclude or push out participation by disenfranchising felons, requiring bureaucratic registration or ID requirements, and more. Thank you to Karen Zaino for reminding me that disengagement may not lie squarely on the shoulders of the citizens themselves.

18. Foa and Mounk, "The Danger of Deconsolidation," 10.

19. William Galston, *Anti-Pluralism: The Populist Threat to Liberal Democracy* (New Haven, CT: Yale University Press, 2018), 12.

20. Richard Wike, Katie Simmon, Bruce Stokes, and Janell Fetterolf, "Globally, Broad Support for Representative and Direct Democracy," *Pew Research Center*, October 16, 2017, http://www.pewglobal.org/2017/10/16/globally-broad-support-for-representative-and-direct-democracy/; Larry Diamond, "Facing up to the Democratic Recession," *Journal of Democracy*, 26, no. 1 (2015): 141–155, 151.

21. Richard Wike, Katie Simmon, Bruce Stokes, and Janell Fetterolf, "Globally, Broad Support for Representative and Direct Democracy," *Pew Research Center*, October 16, 2017, http://www.pewglobal.org/2017/10/16/globally-broad-support-for-representative-and-direct-democracy/

22. Ibid.

23. "Millennials Deeply Uncertain about Democracy Post-Election, But Few Believe It Is in Peril," The Center for Information & Research on Civic Learning and Engagement, April 12, 2017, https://civicyouth.org/millennials-deeply-uncertain-about-democracy-post-election-but-few-believe-it-is-in-peril/.

24. Amy C. Alexander and Christian Welzel, "The Myth of Deconsolidation: Rising Liberalism and the Populist Reaction," *Journal of Democracy*, web exchange (April 28, 2017): 1, https://www.journalofdemocracy.org/sites/default/files/media/Journal%20of%20Democracy%20Web%20Exchange%20-%20Alexander%20and%20Welzel.pdf.

25. Pippa Norris, "Is Western Democracy Backsliding? Diagnosing the Risks," *Journal of Democracy*, web exchange (April 28, 2017): 3, https://www.journalofdemocracy.org/sites/default/files/media/Journal%20of%20Democracy%20Web%20Exchange%20-%20Norris_0.pdf.

26. Alexander and Welzel, "The Myth of Deconsolidation," 2.

27. Ghassan Hage, *Against Paranoid Nationalism: Searching for Hope in a Shrinking Society* (London: Pluto Press, 2003), 20–21; Arlie Russell Hochschild, *Strangers in Their Own Land: Anger and Mourning on the American Right* (New York: New Press, 2018), 226.

28. Alan Mittleman, *Hope in a Democratic Age: Philosophy, Religion, and Political Theory* (Oxford: Oxford University Press, 2009), 21.

29. I'm speaking here of what Peter Drahos calls "public hope" in "Trading in Public Hope," *Annals of the American Academy of Political and Social Science*, 592, no. 1 (2004): 18–38.

30. Galston, *Anti-Pluralism*, 14.

31. I was reminded by my colleague, Whitney Gaskins, that these feelings of let-down are nothing new to African American and other minority groups in the United States, rather it is now becoming more widespread among white and dominant groups who historically were well served and satisfied by democracy and its leaders.

32. Sean Ginwright, *Hope and Healing in Urban Education: How Urban Activists and Teachers Are Reclaiming Matters of the Heart* (New York: Routledge, 2016), 4, 16.

33. Calvin Warren, "Black Nihilism and the Politics of Hope," *CR: The New Centennial Review*, 15 (2015): 215–248; Shannon Sullivan, "Setting Aside Hope: A Pragmatist Approach to Racial Justice," in *Pragmatism and Justice*, edited by Susan Dielman, David Rondel, and Christopher Voparil (Oxford: Oxford University Press, 2017).

34. Warren, "Black Nihilism and the Politics of Hope," 215–248. Tara Yosso describes one such practice in terms of aspirational capital within the LatinX and other communities of color, where members turn to each other to maintain a positive outlook in the face of barriers. Yosso, "Whose Culture Has Capital? A Critical Race Theory Discussion of Community Cultural Wealth," *Race Ethnicity and Education*, 8, no. 1 (2005): 69–91.

35. Jerome Groopman, *The Anatomy of Hope: How People Prevail in the Face of Illness* (New York: Random House, 2004), 179.

36. Ginwright, *Hope and Healing in Urban Education*, 4.

37. Carol Graham, *Happiness for All? Unequal Hopes and Lives in Pursuit of the American Dream* (Princeton, NJ: Princeton University Press, 2017), 19–20; Howard Rhodes, "Despair, Democratic Hope, and Donald Trump," *Religion and Ethics News Weekly*, PBS, November 14, 2016; J. D. Vance describes the findings of the Pew Economic Mobility Project in *Hillbilly Elegy: A Memoir of a Family and Culture in Crisis* (New York: Harper, 2018), 194.

38. Eddie S. Glaude Jr., *Democracy in Black: How Race Still Enslaves the American Soul* (New York: Crown, 2016), 23.

39. I'm borrowing heavily from Glaude, *Democracy in Black*, here.

40. Recent federal law (Every Student Succeeds Act) now requires all schools to assess at least one nonacademic measurement. Grit, believed to be measurable, appeals to some schools and states as a worthy choice. "Every Student Succeeds Act (2015–S. 1177)," GovTrack.us, accessed May 22, 2018, https://www.govtrack.us/congress/bills/114/s1177; Sarah D. Sparks, "'Nation's Report Card' to Gather Data on Grit, Mindset," *Education Week*, June 2, 2015, http://www.edweek.org/ew/articles/2015/06/03/nations-report-card-to-gather-data-on.html.

41. Sheila Suess Kennedy, *Distrust: American Style* (New York: Prometheus Books, 2009).

42. Mark Warren, *Democracy and Trust* (New York: Cambridge University Press, 1999), 12.

43. Peter Levine and Kei Dawashima-Ginsberg, "The Republic Is (Still) at Risk—and Civics Is Part of the Solution," *Medford: Tufts University*, September 21, 2017, 1, http://www.civxsummit.org/documents/v1/SummitWhitePaper.pdf.

44. Susan Page, "Poll: Most Want Obama, GOP to Work Together," *USA Today*, last modified January 18, 2011, http://usatoday30.usatoday.com/news/washington/2011-01-17-poll-obama-house_N.htm; Neil Howe and Reena Nadler, *Yes We Can: The Emergence of Millennials as a Political Generation* (Washington D.C.: New America Foundation, 2009), https://www.lifecourse.com/assets/files/yes_we_can.pdf; Carroll Doherty, "Key Findings on Americans' Views of the U.S. Political System and Democracy," *Pew Research Center*, April 26, 2018, http://www.pewresearch.org/fact-tank/2018/04/26/key-findings-on-americans-views-of-the-u-s-political-system-and-democracy/.

45. I'm thinking here of neoliberal responsibility to fight for one's own self-interest as well as the particular style of "never surrender" negotiation promoted by President Trump.

46. Levine and Dawashima-Ginsberg, "The Republic Is (Still) at Risk," 2.

47. Theda Skocpol, "From Membership to Advocacy," in *Democracies in Flux*, edited by Robert Putnam (New York: Oxford University Press, 2002), 103–136, 105.

48. Theda Skocpol, *Diminished Democracy* (Norman: University of Oklahoma Press, 2003), 178, 214.

49. Ibid.

50. Christopher LeBron, "Equality from a Human Point of View," *Critical Philosophy of Race*, 2, no. 2 (2014): 125–159.

51. Black Lives Matter has wisely been working to expose those differences of experiences in democracy.

52. Mounk, *The People vs Democracy*, 99.

53. Diamond, "Facing up to the Democratic Recession," 148; Roderick P. Hart, *Civic Hope: How Ordinary Americans Keep Democracy Alive* (Cambridge: Cambridge University Press, 2018), 16.

54. Thanks to Melissa Knueven for pointing out this response arising out of a position of power.

55. Ronald Aronson, *We: Reviving Social Hope* (Chicago, IL: University of Chicago Press, 2017), 113.

56. Rhitu Chatterjee, "Americans Are a Lonely Lot, and Young People Bear the Heaviest Burden," *National Public Radio*, May 1, 2018, https://www.npr.org/sections/health-shots/2018/05/01/606588504/americans-are-a-lonely-lot-and-young-people-bear-the-heaviest-burden.

57. "Millennials' Diverse Political Views," Center for Information & Research on Civic Learning and Engagement, March 2018, https://civicyouth.org/wp-content/uploads/2018/02/millennials_diverse_political_views.pdf; "Average Citizen Can Influence Politics," GSS Data Explorer, accessed May 22, 2018, https://gssdataexplorer.norc.org/trends/Politics?measure=poleff3; Richard Wike, Janell Fetterolf, and Bridget Parker, "Even in Era of Disillusionment, Many around the World Say Ordinary Citizens Can Influence Government," *Pew Research Center*, October 24, 2016, http://www.pewglobal.org/2016/10/24/

even-in-era-of-disillusionment-many-around-the-world-say-ordinary-citizens-can-influence-government/.

58. Aronson, *We: Reviving Social Hope.*

59. Tyler Cowen, *The Complacent Class: The Self-Defeating Quest for the American Dream* (New York: St Martin's Press, 2017), 194.

60. While this is a controversial take on poor and working-class whites in America, J. D. Vance argues that those people in particular are experiencing a sort of despair that combines pessimism and estrangement. And he argues that those people lack agency, feeling little control over their own lives. Vance, *Hillbilly Elegy*, 194.

61. M. Gilens and B. Page, "Testing Theories of American Politics: Elites, Interest Groups, and Average Citizens," *Perspectives on Politics* (2014): 564–581.

62. Deva Woodly, "#BlackLivesMatter and the Democratic Necessity of Social Movements," *Columbia Center for Contemporary Critical Thought Blog*, November 1, 2017.

63. For more on this temptation, see Jeffrey Stout in *Blessed Are the Organized: Grassroots Democracy in America* (Princeton, NJ: Princeton University Press, 2010).

Chapter 2

64. Darren Webb, "Pedagogies of Hope," *Studies in Philosophy and Education*, 32 (2013): 397–414, 398.

65. Psychologist Richard Davidson noted in Groopman, *Anatomy of Hope*, 193.

66. Adrienne Martin, "Hopes and Dreams 1," *Philosophy and Phenomenological Research*, 83, no. 1 (2011): 148–173.

67. This view is most pronounced in the subfield of psychology known as positive psychology, which is rooted in the work of C. R. Snyder.

68. Joseph Godfrey traces this religious view in *A Philosophy of Human Hope* (Boston: Martinus Nijhoff Publishers, 1987), as does Allan Mittleman in *Hope in a Democratic Age: Philosophy, Religion, and Political Theory* (Oxford: Oxford University Press, 2009).

69. I thank my colleague, Whitney Gaskins, for pointing out that black churches, while sometimes guided by the tendencies of theologians I noted, often actually teach about hope much differently. Rather than focusing on God as Savior, who intervenes on our behalf, many black churches emphasize God as Provider of the resources we need to help ourselves pursue more fulfilling lives. And they emphasize helping one another. Anne Streaty Winberly and Sarah Frances Farmer further describe black youth ministries as helping youth envision and claim a positive future in *Raising Hope: 4 Paths to Courageous Living for Black Youth* (Kansas City, MO: Wesley's Foundry Books, 2017).

70. For more along these lines, see the work of Gabriel Marcel and Joseph Godfrey.

71. Cheshire Calhoun, chapter 5 draft on hope, http://cheshirecalhoun.com/wp-content/uploads/2013/05/Ch5Hope.doc.pdf, 25.

72. Myths of racial justice and equality have been used in this optimistic way to hide ongoing injustice and to assure members of racial minority groups that life will improve.

Sometimes this is done by highlighting exceptional individuals who have overcome structural inequality by supposedly pulling themselves up by their bootstraps as evidence for optimism.

73. Groopman, *Anatomy of Hope*, 199.
74. Patrick A. Shade, *Habits of Hope: A Pragmatic Theory of the Life of Hope* (Nashville, TN: Vanderbilt University Press, 2001), 60. For Shade, hope entails relationships with other people which may support us and which may develop skills and abilities that can help us in our personal endeavors (111). While Shade does briefly allude to communities that may nurture the hopes of individuals, I aim to go further in theorizing and valuing the social and political aspects of hope. Whereas he does quickly consider communities as sources of hope for individuals, he doesn't explore the role of hope within democratic life or how hoping together may work for citizens. My pragmatist account of hope as habits is more thoroughly and intentionally social and political.
75. I aim to go beyond the theory of Patrick Shade, who has already sketched an initial pragmatist vision of hope. Whereas he sometimes constrains his portrayal of hope to the life of the individual, I aim to describe explicitly social and political aspects of hope.
76. In this regard, it is more akin to the spirit of social hope, which other pragmatists, such as Judith Green, have suggested but have not fleshed out in detail regarding its cultivation or its role in democracy. Judith M. Green, *Pragmatism and Social Hope: Deepening Democracy in Global Contexts* (New York: Columbia University Press, 2008).
77. The historian William Goetzmann, *Beyond the Revolution: A History of American Thought from Paine to Pragmatism* (New York: Basic Books, 2009), 5.
78. Joan Richardson, *Pragmatism and American Experience* (Cambridge: Cambridge University Press, 2014), ix.
79. John Dewey's 1903 statement as captured in Richard Rorty, *Philosophy and Social Hope* (New York: Penguin Books, 1999), 120.
80. Robert Westbrook, *Democratic Hope: Pragmatism and the Politics of Truth* (Ithaca, NY: Cornell University Press, 2005), 204.
81. Goetzmann, *Beyond the Revolution*, 47.
82. I'm not saying that pragmatists always carefully attend to those differences based on race and class, for far too few have. But I am saying that pragmatism creates a space for and calls for those aspects of social and political life to be considered and reconstructed.
83. John Dewey, "The Public and Its Problems," in *John Dewey: The Later Works, 1925–1953*, vol. 2, edited by J. A. Boydston (Carbondale: Southern Illinois University Press, 1984), 235–372, 350.
84. Raphael C. Allison, "Walt Whitman, William James, and Pragmatist Aesthetics," *Walt Whitman Quarterly Review*, 20, no. 1 (2002): 19–29, 25–27.
85. Louis Menand, *The Metaphysical Club: A Story of Ideas in America* (Boston: Farrar, Straus and Giroux, 2002), 89.
86. James T. Kloppenberg, "James's *Pragmatism* and American Culture, 1907–2007," In *100 Years of Pragmatism*, edited by John Stuhr (Bloomington: Indiana University Press, 2010), 7–40, 21.

87. Colin Koopman, "Pragmatism as a Philosophy of Hope: Emerson, James, Dewey, Rorty," *Journal of Speculative Philosophy*, 20, no. 2 (2006): 106–116, 113.

88. Ibid., 106.

89. Elizabeth Cooke, "Transcendental Hope: Peirce, Hookway, and Pihlström on the Conditions for Inquiry," *Transactions of the Charles S. Peirce Society, 41*, no. 3 (summer 2005): 651–674, 655; Charles Sanders Peirce, *The Essential Peirce, Vol. 2: Selected Philosophical Writings (1893–1913)*, edited by Peirce Edition Project (Bloomington: Indiana University Press), 106.

90. Charles Sanders Peirce, *Collected Papers of Charles Sanders Peirce, Volumes 5–6*, edited by Charles Hartshorne and Paul Weiss (Cambridge, MA: Belknap Press of Harvard University Press, 1934/1935), 222.

91. Charles Sanders Peirce, *The Essential Peirce, Vol. 1: Selected Philosophical Writings (1867–1893)*, edited by N. Houser and C. Kloesel (Bloomington: Indiana University Press, 1878 [1992]).

92. John Dewey, "Democracy and Education," in *The Collected Works of John Dewey, 1882–1953: The Middle Works, 1899–1924*, vol. 9, edited by J. A. Boydston (Carbondale and Edwardsville: Southern Illinois University Press, 1980), 55.

93. Stephen M. Fishman and Lucille Parkinson McCarthy, *John Dewey and the Philosophy and Practice of Hope* (Urbana: University of Illinois Press, 2007), 12.

94. Fishman and McCarthy, *John Dewey and the Philosophy and Practice of Hope*, 5.

95. Bernard P. Dauenhauer, *Elements of Responsible Politics* (Boston: Kluwer Academic Publishers, 1991), 121.

96. Shade, *Habits of Hope*, 94.

97. Richard Rorty, *Philosophy and Social Hope* (New York: Penguin Books, 1999), 120.

98. Charles Sanders Peirce, "How To Make Our Ideas Clear," In *The Essential Peirce*, vol. 1, edited by N. Houser and C. Kloesel (Bloomington: Indiana University Press, 1878/1992), 124–141.

99. Charlene Haddock Seigfried, *William James's Radical Reconstruction of Philosophy* (Albany: State University of New York Press, 1990), 294.

100. I'm drawing closely here on an account of pragmatist truth and flourishing that I detailed in *Breaking Bad Habits of Race and Gender: Transforming Identity in Schools* (Lanham, MD: Rowman & Littlefield Press, 2008).

101. William James, "Lecture VI: Pragmatism's Conception of Truth," In *Pragmatism: A New Name for Some Old Ways of Thinking* (Online: Project Gutenberg EBook, 2013 [1907]), http://www.gutenberg.org/files/5116/5116-h/5116-h.htm.

102. Koopman, "Pragmatism as a Philosophy of Hope," 109.

103. Richard Rorty, "Universality and Truth," in *Rorty and His Critics*, edited by R. Brandom (Oxford: Blackwell, 2000), 3.

104. Lynn Baker, "'Just Do It': Pragmatism and Progressive Social Change," in *Pragmatism in Law and Society*, edited by Michael Brint and William Weaver (Boulder, CO: Westview Press, 1991), 101.

105. Rorty, "Pragmatism, Relativism, and Irrationalism," *Proceedings and Addresses of the American Philosophical Association*, 53, no. 6 (1980), 166.

106. Green, *Pragmatism and Social Hope*, 107.

107. Joseph Winters is also concerned with Rorty's inattentiveness to the substantial harmful history of racism as he focuses on American pride and progress in *Hope Draped in Black: Race, Melancholy, and the Agony of Progress* (Durham, NC: Duke University Press, 2016), 213.

108. For more, see my review of Judith Green's book on hope: Sarah M. Stitzlein, "Reviving Social Hope and Pragmatism in Troubling Times," *Journal of Philosophy of Education, 43*, no. 4 (2009): 657–663.

109. Green, *Pragmatism and Social Hope*, 23.

110. Dewey, "Democracy and Education," 294.

111. Thanks to the social studies educator and critical theorist Lisa Sibbett, for her helpful commentary on this section.

112. This is especially the case with readers influenced by the critical arguments of Michelle Alexander, Charles Mills, and Derrick Bell.

113. I recognize that many developments, improvements, and signs of progress have been achieved on the backs of some of the most struggling and oppressed people in America and elsewhere. Asserting the "fact" of historical progress may fall prey to or perpetuate "complex relations of domination, exclusion, and silencing of colonized and racialized subjects," especially when not accompanied by a critical and problematizing genealogy. And assessments of progress, even though they should be historically and contextually grounded when possible, may be based on my values or those dominant in America today. For more about these potential problems, see Amy Allen, *The End of Progress* (New York: Columbia University Press, 2015), 19.

114. David Moscrop gets at these sorts of questions in, "If We Don't Rethink the Concept of Progress, It Could Point Society toward Oblivion," *Maclean's*, October 24, 2018, last accessed December 5, 2018, https://www.macleans.ca/opinion/if-we-dont-rethink-the-concept-of-progress-it-could-point-society-toward-oblivion/.

115. Biographer Jon Meacham has expertly laid out examples of how political leaders and citizens have faced periods of divisiveness and fear in America and brought hope that lead the country forward. See *The Soul of America: The Battle for Our Better Angels* (New York: Random House, 2018).

116. Cornel West, "Prisoners of Hope," in *The Impossible Will Take a Little While*, edited by Paul Rogat Loeb (Cambridge, MA: Basic Books, 2004), 296.

117. Aronson, *We: Reviving Social Hope*, 92.

118. John Dewey, "Contributions to 'A Cyclopedia of Education,' Volumes 3, 4, and 5," *John Dewey: The Middle Works, 1899–1924, Volume 7: 1912–1914*, edited by J. A. Boydston (Carbondale: Southern Illinois University Press, 1979), 294.

119. I describe the preservation of the status quo in chapter 5, where I discuss some of the problems with focusing on grit rather than hope.

120. Westbrook, *Democratic Hope*, 205.

121. John Dewey, "Essays, Miscellany, and Reconstruction in Philosophy," in *The Middle Works (1899–1924)*, vol. 12, edited by J. A. Boydston (Carbondale: Southern Illinois University Press, 1982), 181–182.

122. Notably, Reverend King borrowed these words from Theodore Parker.

123. Dewey, "Essays, Miscellany, and Reconstruction in Philosophy," 77.

124. I'm reminded here of Colin Koopman's related point: "This is what it means to take a melioristic perspective on truth. Meliorism focuses on improvements that are due to our energies and efforts. Truth, understood melioristically, is an improvement resulting from our work." Koopman, "Pragmatism as a Philosophy of Hope," 22.

125. Stephane Madelrieux, "Pragmatism: The Task before Us (A review of Koopman's *Pragmatism as Transition*), *Contemporary Pragmatism*, 14 (2017): 203–211.

126. Michael Kempa, "A Museum of Hope: A Story of Robben Island," *Annals of the American Academy of Political and Social Science*, 592, no. 1 (March 2004).

127. I'm following Judith Green here, *Pragmatism and Social Hope*, 78–79.

128. Thank you to Lori Foote for pointing out the multiple aspects of agency at work here.

129. Thanks again to Lisa Sibbett for reminding me of the troubling findings of disparity and lack of influence noted by Martin Gilens and Benjamin I. Page, "Testing Theories of American Politics: Elites, Interest Groups, and Average Citizens," *Perspectives on Politics*, 12, no. 3 (2014): 564–581.

130. Koopman, "Pragmatism as a Philosophy of Hope," 107.

131. Ibid., 207

132. Ibid., 112.

Chapter 3

133. James W. Fraser and others have suggested that hope can be chosen over despair. *A History of Hope* (New York: Palgrave MacMillan, 2002), xiv.

134. Dewey, "Democracy and Education," 199–200.

135. Dewey, "Democracy and Education," 53.

136. John Dewey, "Human Nature and Conduct," *John Dewey, The Middle Works, 1899–1924, Volume 14: 1922*, edited by J. A. Boydston (Carbondale: Southern Illinois University Press, 1983), 67.

137. Ibid., 124.

138. Ibid., 21.

139. Dewey, "Democracy and Education," 54.

140. Ibid.

141. Stitzlein, *Breaking Bad Habits of Race and Gender*.

142. Dewey, "Human Nature and Conduct," 52.

143. I'm borrowing this example from my book *American Public Education and the Responsibility of Its Citizens* (New York: Oxford University Press, 2017).

144. Dewey, "Democracy and Education," 48.

145. John Dewey, "The Need for a Recovery of Philosophy," *John Dewey, The Middle Works, 1899-1924, Volume 10: 1916-1917*, edited by J. A. Boydston (Carbondale: Southern Illinois University Press, 1983), 50.

146. Joseph Godfrey similarly and rightfully points out that hope implies evaluation about possibility and the soundness of our desires. Godfrey, *A Philosophy of Human Hope*, 169.

147. John Dewey, "The Nature of Deliberation," *John Dewey, The Middle Works, 1899–1924, Volume 14: 1922,* edited by J. A. Boydston (Carbondale: Southern Illinois University Press, 1983), 132.

148. Shade, "Habits of Hope," 6–7.

149. Ibid.

150. John Dewey, "Experience and Nature," *John Dewey, The Later Works, 1925–1983: Volume 1: 1925,* edited by J. A. Boydston (Carbondale: Southern Illinois University Press, 1983), 325.

151. Michael Eldridge, *Transforming Experience: John Dewey's Cultural Instrumentalism* (Nashville, TN: Vanderbilt University Press, 1998), 198.

152. Shane J. Lopez, *Making Hope Happen* (New York: Atria Books, 2013), 79.

153. Aronson, *Reviving Social Hope,* 47–48

154. Dewey, "Creative Democracy," 226.

155. Lia Haro, "The Affective Politics of Insurgent Hope," in *Hope against Hope,* edited by Janet Horrigan and Ed Wiltse (Amsterdam: Rodopi, 2010), 200.

156. Dewey, "Democracy and Education," 182.

157. Green, *Pragmatism and Social Hope,* 129.

158. Karen Tumulty, "How Donald Trump Came up with 'Make America Great Again,'" *Washington Post,* January 18, 2017, https://www.washingtonpost.com/politics/how-donald-trump-came-up-with-make-america-great-again/2017/01/17/fb6acf5e-dbf7-11e6-ad42-f3375f271c9c_story.html?utm_term=.b5baf59f814c.

159. Some citizens did ask "Great for whom?" and noted how they struggled to identify the time that America was great for all people that Trump was referring to. A few included: Cyneatha Millsaps, "Make America Great—again?" *The Mennonite,* January 16, 2017, https://themennonite.org/opinion/make-america-great/; Maegan Vazquez, "NY Gov. Andrew Cuomo Says America 'Was Never That Great,'" *CNN,* August 16, 2018, https://www.cnn.com/2018/08/15/politics/andrew-cuomo-america-was-never-that-great/index.html; Jill Filipovic, "The Major Problem with 'Make America Great Again,'" *Cosmopolitan,* March 16, 2018, https://www.cosmopolitan.com/politics/a55305/make-america-great-again-donald-trump/.

160. Melissa Knueven rightfully pointed out to the me the hats were used not just to identify like-minded citizens but perhaps also to explicitly distance wearers from political opponents and maybe even to excite more polarization and opposition between the two.

161. I borrow these phrases inspired by Ernst Bloch from Andre Willis, Templeton Foundation Conference on Hope and Optimism, Estes Park, Colorado, June 2016.

162. Akiba Lerner, *Redemptive Hope: From the Age of Enlightenment to the Age of Obama* (New York: Fordham University Press, 2015), 90–91.

163. Victoria McGreer, "The Art of Good Hope," *Annals of the American Academy of Political and Social Science,* 592, no. 1 (2004): 100–137, 123.

164. Victoria McGreer, "Trust, Hope, and Empowerment," *Australian Journal of Philosophy,* 86, no. 2 (2008): 237–254, 247–248.

165. Jayne M. Waterworth, *A Philosophical Analysis of Hope* (New York: Palgrave Macmillan, 2004), 84–85.

166. Charley Taylor, *Sources of the Self: The Making of Modern Identity* (Cambridge, MA: Harvard University Press, 1989)and Augusta Moore, "Diversity in Deliberation: The Importance of Responsiveness and Respect," American Educational Research Association, New York City, April 2017.

167. Brett Johnson, "Overcoming 'Doom and Gloom': Empowering Students in Courses on Social Problems, Injustice, and Inequality," *Teaching Sociology*, 33, no. 1 (2005): 44–58.

168. Adrienne Martin, *How We Hope: A Moral Psychology* (Princeton, NJ: Princeton University Press, 2013), 32.

169. Cornel West, *Hope on a Tightrope* (Carlsbad, CA: Smiley Books, 2008), 216.

170. Ibid., 41.

171. Ibid., 217.

172. Ibid.

173. Ibid., 6.

174. Cornel West, "The Limits of Neopragmatism," in *Pragmatism in Law and Society*, edited by Michael Brindt and William Weaver (Boulder, CO: Westview Press, 1991), 125.

175. Ibid.

176. West, *Hope on a Tightrope*, 22.

177. R. L. Stephens, "The Birthmark of Damnation: Ta-Nehisi Coates and the Black Body," *Viewpoint Magazine*, May 22, 2017, https://www.viewpointmag.com/2017/05/17/the-birthmark-of-damnation-ta-nehisi-coates-and-the-black-body/; Melvin Rogers, "Keeping the Faith," *Boston Review*, November 1, 2017, accessed November 10, 2018, http://bostonreview.net/race/melvin-rogers-keeping-faith.

178. Ta-Nehisi Coates, *Between the World and Me* (New York: Spiegel and Grau, 2015), 151.

179. Ibid., 120, 12.

180. Glaude, *Democracy in Black*, 126.

181. Ibid., 125.

182. Ta-Nehisi Coates, "Hope and the Historian," *The Atlantic*, December 11, 2015, https://www.theatlantic.com/politics/archive/2015/12/hope-and-the-historian/419961/.

183. Ezra Klein, "Ta-Nehisi Coates Is Not Here to Comfort You," *Vox*, October 9, 2017, https://www.vox.com/2017/10/9/16430390/ta-nehisi-coates-podcast-hope-book.

184. Rogers, "Keeping the Faith."

185. Joseph Winters, *Hope Draped in Black* (Durham, NC: Duke University Press, 2016), 213.

186. Martin Luther King Jr., "Eulogy for the Martyred Children," Birmingham Campaign, September 18, 1963, https://kinginstitute.stanford.edu/king-papers/documents/eulogy-martyred-children.

187. Martin Luther King Jr., *A Christmas Sermon on Peace*, CBC Learning Systems, 1965.

188. Glaude, *Democracy in Black*, 98.

189. Calvin Warren, "Black Nihilism and the Politics of Hope," *CR: The New Centennial Review*, 15, no. 1 (2015): 215–248; Shannon Sullivan, "Setting Aside Hope: A

Pragmatist Approach to Racial Justice," in *Pragmatism and Justice*, edited by Susan Dieleman, David Rondel, and Christopher Voparil (New York: Oxford University Press, 2017).

190. Warren, "Black Nihilism and the Politics of Hope," 245.

191. Shane J. Lopez, *Making Hope Happen* (New York: Atria Books, 2013), 18.

192. Thanks to Lisa Sibbett for her helpful shaping of this paragraph.

193. Doug Lederman, "Is Higher Education Really Losing the Public?" *Inside Higher Education*, December 15, 2017, and Eric Kelderman, " 'Higher Education' Isn't so Popular, Poll Finds, but Local Colleges Get Lots of Love," *Chronicle of Higher Education*, May 21, 2018.

194. Pew Research, "Mixed Messages about Public Trust in Science," December 8, 2017, and Gleb Tsipursky, "(Dis)trust in Science," *Scientific American Blog*, July 5, 2018.

Chapter 4

195. Bonnie Honig rightly describes real public things. She warns, "without them democratic life is not just impoverished but unsustainable. If democratic theorists neglect public things, we end up theorizing the demos or proceduralism without the things that give them purpose and whose adhesive and integrative powers are necessary to the perpetual reformation of democratic collectivity." Bonnie Honig, *Public Things: Democracy in Disrepair*. New York: Fordham University Press, 2017.

196. I follow J. J. Godfrey in *A Philosophy of Human Hope*; Jayne Waterworth in *A Philosophical Analysis of Hope*; and others in using this distinction between objects and objectives of hope.

197. For details on how Dewey links indeterminate situations, desire, and objects of hope, see John Dewey, "Desire and Intelligence," *John Dewey, The Middle Works, 1899–1924, Volume 14: 1922*, edited by J. A. Boydston (Carbondale: Southern Illinois University Press, 1983), 172.

198. Personal communication July 6, 2016, regarding handout distributed at the Templeton Foundation Hope Conference in Estes Park, Colorado, in June 2016.

199. For more on joint commitments, see Margaret Gilbert, *Joint Commitment: How We Make the Social World* (Oxford: Oxford University Press, 2013).

200. McGreet, Victoria. "The Art of Good Hope," *The Annals of the American Academy*, March 2004: 100–137.

201. Note how this differs from the sort of hope often demonstrated by politicians, where they assert objects that the public may not actually endorse or understand then uphold them beyond question. See Peter Drahos, "Trading in Public Hope," in *Annals of the American Academy of Political and Social Science*, 592, no. 1 (2004).

202. For more see Margaret Gilbert, "Rationality in Collective Action," *Philosophy of the Social Sciences*, 36, no. 1 (2006): 3–17, 11.

203. William James, *Pragmatism: A New Name for Some Old Ways of Thinking*, lecture 2 (New York: Longmans, 1907).

204. See similar concerns expressed by Hannah Arendt in Alan Mittleman, *Hope in a Democratic Age*, 197; and by Aronson, *Reviving Social Hope*, 157; and by Sullivan, *Pragmatism and Justice*, 3.

205. For more about this interpretation of Dewey, see Stephen M. Fishman and L. McCarthy, *John Dewey and the Philosophy and Practice of Hope* (Urbana: University of Illinois Press, 2007), 21, 51, 83.

206. Shade, "Habits of Hope," 31.

207. Ibid., 71.

208. Ibid., 19, 36.

209. Kloppenberg, James. *Reading Obama* (Princton, NJ: Princeton University Press, 2011), 163, and Dauenhauer, *Elements of Responsible Politics*, 136, 139.

210. This paragraph is heavily aligned with the ideas expressed by Yone Appelbaum, "Is the American Idea Doomed?" *The Atlantic*, November 2017, https://www.theatlantic.com/magazine/archive/2017/11/is-the-american-idea-over/540651/.

211. Olivia Paschal, "Read John McCain's Final Letter to America," *The Atlantic*, September 4, 2018, https://www.theatlantic.com/politics/archive/2018/08/john-mccains-final-letter-to-america/568669/?utm_source=fbb.

212. Note here that I'm not saying we must tolerate all views or all ways of life; certainly there are some that should be squelched. I'm speaking of tolerance of a wide array of ways of living in general.

213. Green, *Pragmatism and Social Hope*, 105.

214. Adam Kadlac, "The Virtue of Hope," *Ethical Theory and Moral Practice*, 18 (2015): 337–354, 350.

215. Clinton: "Address Accepting the Presidential Nomination."

216. It should not be lost in this discussion that these sorts of ideas also fed a lot of political divisiveness during the election, as Melissa Knueven reminded me.

217. I recognize that she was received in quite a polarizing way once elected, but my focus here is more on what led to her run and the movement that build around it.

218. For more defending this aspect of democracy, see Paul Fairchild, *Why Democracy?* Albany, NY: State University Press, 2008.

219. I am aware that this suggestion may seem to border on indoctrination, which feels anathema to democracy. I don't mean for it to be done in a straightforward and unquestioning way, but rather to highlight its benefits more, while also talking about its weaknesses.

220. Peter Berger, *The Many Altars of Modernity: Toward a Paradigm for Religion in a Pluralist Age* (Boston: De Gruyter Mouton, 2014).

221. For more, see Michael Lamb, "Aquinas and the Virtues of Hope: Theological and Democratic," *Journal of Religious Ethics*, 44, no. 2 (2016): 300–332.

222. These compose what Oliver Bennett calls the "democratic promise." Bennett, *Cultures of Optimism* (New York: Palgrave Macmillan, 2015).

223. David Halpin, *Hope and Education: The Role of the Utopian Imagination* (New York: Routledge Falmer, 2003), 15.

224. John Dewey, *Art as Experience* (New York: Penguin Books, 1932), 360.

225. Michael Walzer, *Toward a Global Civil Society* (Providence, RI: Berghahn Books, 1998), 239.

226. For more on the importance, practice, and development of political dissent, see Sarah M. Stitzlein, *Teaching for Dissent: Citizenship Education and Political Activism* (New York: Routledge, 2014).

227. I also want to note the example of Ferguson protest leader, Deray McKesson, who not only exhibited hope but also described a similar pragmatist spirit in *On the Other Side of Freedom: The Case for Hope* (New York: Penguin Random House, 2018).

228. Association for Supervision and Curriculum Development Smart Brief Survey, March 7, 2019.

229. Marley Jay, "Six Months of #MeToo: Hopes Are High for Lasting Impact," *The Mercury News*, March 31, 2018, accessed August 15, 2018, https://www.mercurynews.com/2018/03/31/six-months-of-metoo-hopes-are-high-for-lasting-impact/.

230. Aisha Harris, "She Founded Me Too: Now She Wants to Move Past the Trauma," *New York Times*, October 15, 2018, https://www.nytimes.com/2018/10/15/arts/tarana-burke-metoo-anniversary.html?smid=nytcore-ios-share&fbclid=IwAR0zoh6C9hC0IsHk751PVHBLqiq3_ynWtwuVGqCJuJpAGRs0EXnIUHmm4cc.

231. For an account of the experience of being cheated and left behind, see Arlie Russell Hoschschild, *Strangers in Their Own Land*.

232. For more along these lines, see Woodly, "#BlackLivesMatter and the Democratic Necessity of Social Movements."

233. Shade, *Habits of Hope*, x.

234. James D. Anderson has been significant in the unearthing and retelling of these stories in multiple contexts and outlets.

235. James W. Fraser highlights the story of women's suffrage in *A History of Hope*.

236. Walt Whitman, "Democratic Vistas," in *Two Rivulets* (Camden, NJ: New Republic Print, 1876), 37.

237. I'm drawing here on Cheshire Calhoun's notion of hope narratives. Cheshire Calhoun, "Hope," 25, available at http://cheshirecalhoun.com/wp-content/uploads/2013/05/Ch5Hope.doc.pdf.

238. PlaceBase Productions, accessed August 15, 2018, http://placebaseproductions.com/.

239. I'm drawing here on Josiah Royce, whom John Kaag nicely summarizes in *American Philosophy: A Love Story* (New York: Farrar, Straus and Giroux, 2016).

240. Luc Bovens, "The Value of Hope," *Philosophy and Phenomenological Research*, 59 (1999): 676.

241. Calhoun, "Hope," 23.

242. Dewey, *The Public and Its Problems*, 15–16.

243. Aronson, *We: Reviving Social Hope*, 156.

244. Claudia Blöser and Titus Stahl, "Fundamental Hope and Practical Identity," *Philosophical Papers*, 46, no. 3 (2017): 345–371.

Chapter 5

245. Julian Edgoose (2010) has previously described the history of viewing schooling as hopeful in this journal via the work of David Tyack and Larry Cuban, "Hope in the Unexpected: How Can Teachers Still Make a Difference in the World?" *Teachers College Record*, 112, no. 2: 386–406.

246. Valerie J. Calderon and Tim Hodges, "K-12 Leaders: Student Engagement, Hope Top Measures of a School," *Gallup*, http://www.gallup.com/opinion/gallup/188012/leaders-student-engagement-hope-top-measures-school.aspx?g_source=CATEGORY_EDUCATION&g_medium=topic&g_campaign=tiles.

247. "Brentwood High School: A School of Hope," May 2010, *Principal Leadership*, 10, no. 9: 14–18.

248. Madeline Sackler, *The Lottery*, Documentary, Great Curve Films, 2010; Davis Guggenheim, *Waiting for Superman*, Documentary, Paramount Vantage, 2010.

249. Julian Edgoose, "Hope in the Unexpected: How Can Teachers Still Make a Difference in the World?," *Teachers College Record*, 112, no. 2 (2010): 386–406.

250. Valerie J. Calderon, and Daniela Yu., "8 Things You Need to Know about Students," Gallup.com, May 25, 2017, accessed September 6, 2018, http://news.gallup.com/opinion/gallup/211028/eight-things-need-know-students.aspx?g_source=link_NEWSV9&g_medium=TOPIC&g_campaign=item_&g_content=8. Admittedly, this sort of hope is different from the social and political hoping I've been describing, but there are certainly connections between the two.

251. Ibid.

252. Phi Delta Kappan Annual Poll, http://pdkpoll.pdkintl.org/; Jennifer L. Hochschild and Nathan B. Scovronick, *The American Dream and the Public Schools* (Oxford: Oxford University Press, 2003), 11; and Phi Delta Kappan Annual Poll 2016 http://pdkpoll2015.pdkintl.org/581.

253. Diana Owen, "Public Attitudes about Civic Education" (paper presented at the Annual Meeting for the American Political Science Association, Chicago, IL, August 29–September 1, 2013).

254. Dara Zeehandelaar and Amber M. Winkler, *What Parents Want: Education Preferences and Trade-Offs, A National Survey of K-12 Parents* (Washington, DC: Thomas Fordham Institute, 2013).

255. Kit Harris, "ED Pulse Poll Results: What Is the Purpose of Education?" *The Whole Child Blog*, May 6, 2014, last accessed January 30, 2016. http://www.wholechildeducation.org/blog/ed-pulse-poll-results-what-is-the-purpose-of-education

256. William Galston, "Civic Knowledge, Civic Education, and Civic Engagement," in *Fountain of Youth: Strategies and Tactics for Mobilizing America's Young Voters*, edited by Daniel M. Shea and John C. Green (Lanham, MD: Rowman and Littlefield, 2007): 95–114; Allison Penelope Anoll, "Creating Citizens: Civics Education, Civic Socialization and Engagement Patterns," dissertation, College of William and Mary, 2009.

257. Peter Levine describes the history of civics and political science in *The Future of Democracy: Developing the Next Generation of American Citizens* (Medford, MA: Tufts University Press, 2007), 113.

258. Center on Education Policy, 2008, "Instructional Time in Elementary Schools: A Closer Look at Changes for Specific Subjects."

259. Joel Westheimer, "No Child Left Thinking: Democracy At-Risk in American Schools," *Democratic Dialogue Series* 17 (2008): 5. Joseph Kahne and Ellen Middaugh, "Democracy for Some: The Civic Opportunity Gap," In *Engaging Young People in Civic Life*, edited by James Youniss and Peter Levine (Nashville, TN: Vanderbilt University Press, 2009), 29–58, 31. Meira Levinson, *No Citizen Left Behind* (Cambridge, MA: Harvard University Press, 2012).

260. *College, Career & Civic Life C3 Framework for Social Studies State Standards* (Silver Springs, MD: National Council for the Social Studies, 2017), 6.

261. George W. Chilcoat and Jerry A. Ligon, "Issues-Centered Instruction in the Social Studies Classroom: The Richard E. Gross Problem-Solving Approach Model," *Social Studies Review* (2004), 40(1): 40–46.

262. Andrew Tripodo and Robert Pondisco, "Seizing the Civic Education Moment," *Educational Leadership*, 75, no. 3 (2017), accessed September 6, 2018, http://www.ascd.org/publications/educational-leadership/nov17/vol75/num03/Seizing-the-Civic-Education-Moment.aspx.

263. Robert J. Sampson, *Great American City: Chicago and the Enduring Neighborhood Effect* (Chicago, IL: University of Chicago Press, 2012), 168; "CIRCLE Receives W.T. Grant Foundation Support to Study Social and Economic Effects of Youth Civic Empowerment and Participation," CIRCLE, accessed September 6, 2018, https://civicyouth.org/circle-receives-w-t-grant-foundation-support-to-study-social-and-economic-effects-of-youth-civic-empowerment-and-participation/?cat_id=7.

264. Levine, *The Future of Democracy*; Galston, "Civic Knowledge, Civic Education, and Civic Engagement," 113.

265. Michigan Municipal League, "Civic Engagement: Best Practices and Example from across the State" (2017) http://placemaking.mml.org/wp-content/uploads/2013/02/FINAL-MML-2014-Engagement-Booklet.pdf; Ryan T. Knowles, "Teaching Who You Are: Connecting Teachers' Civic Education Ideology to Instructional Strategies," *Theory & Research in Social Education*, 46, no.1 (2018): 68–109, doi: 10.1080/00933104.2017.1356776.

266. "New Tisch College Initiative on Social-Emotional Learning and Civic Engagement," Jonathan M. Tisch College of Civic Life, July 26, 2017, accessed September 6, 2018, https://tischcollege.tufts.edu/news/new-tisch-college-initiative-social-emotional-learning-and-civic-engagement.

267. Howe and Nadler, "Yes We Can,"

268. CIRCLE, https://civicyouth.org/wp-content/uploads/2018/02/millennials_diverse_political_views.pdf and https://civicyouth.org/five-takeaways-on-social-media-and-the-youth-vote-in-2018/, accessed November 28, 2018.

269. Abby Kiesa, Alexander P. Orlowski, Peter Levine, Deborah Both, Emily Hoban Kirby, Mark Hugo Lopez, and Karlo Barrios Marcelo, "Millennials Talk Politics: A Study of College Student Political Engagement" (CIRCLE, 2007), 9.

270. Howe, 3.

271. Kiesa.

272. Mikhail Zinshteyn, "College Freshman Are More Politically Engaged Than They Have Been in Decades," *FiveThirtyEight*, February 11, 2016; and Kevin Eagan et al., "The American Freshman: National Norms Fall 2015," Cooperative Institutional Research Program at UCLA, https://www.heri.ucla.edu/monographs/TheAmericanFreshman2015.pdf.

273. Eagan et al., "The American Freshman."

274. Corey Seemiller and Meghan Grace, "Generation Z: Educating and Engaging the Next Generation of Students," *About Campus* (August 2017): 21–26.

275. Corey Seemiller and Meghan Grace, *Generation Z Goes to College* (San Francisco: John Wiley & Sons, 2016), 23.

276. Tim Carter, "Preparing Generation Z for the Teaching Profession," *SRATE Journal*, 27, no. 1 (2018): 1–8.

277. I'm thankful to Melissa Knueven for helping me understand these changes. See also Monica Jimenez, "Trends in Youth Voting Are Worrying," *Tufts Now*, October 27, 2016; Marjorie Howard, "The High School Roots of Civic Engagement," *Tufts Now*, May 23, 2014; and Zinshteyn, "College Freshmen Are More Politically Engaged."

278. US Department of Education, *Promoting Grit, Tenacity, and Perseverance: Critical Factors for Success in the 21st Century* (2013), http://pgbovine.net/OET-Draft-Grit-Report-2-17-13.pdf; Sarah D. Sparks, "'Nation's Report Card' to Gather Data on Grit, Mindset," *Education Week*, http://www.edweek.org/ew/articles/2015/06/03/nations-report-card-to-gather-data-on.html.

279. Claire Robertson-Kraft and Angela Duckworth, "True Grit: Trait-Level Perseverance and Passion for Long-Term Goals Predicts Effectiveness and Retention among Novice Teachers," *Teachers College Record*, 116, no. 3 (2014): 1–27.

280. Evie Blad, "Walton Family Foundation Invests in Research on Measuring Grit, Character," *Education Week*, September 17, 2015, http://blogs.edweek.org/edweek/rulesforengagement/2015/09/walton_family_foundation_social-emotional_learning.html

281. Angela Duckworth, "Don't Grade Schools on Grit," *New York Times*, March 26, 2016, http://www.nytimes.com/2016/03/27/opinion/sunday/dont-grade-schools-on-grit.html?_r=0.

282. Angela Duckworth, *Grit: The Power of Passion and Perseverance* (New York: Scribner, 2016), 64.

283. Ibid., 64.

284. Ibid., 91–92.

285. Ibid., 148.

286. Duckworth in video "Teaching Grit Cultivates Resilience," available at http://www.bitofgrit.com/home.

287. Duckworth, *Grit*; Paul Tough, *How Children Succeed: Grit, Curiosity, and the Hidden Power of Character* (New York: Houghton Mifflin Harcourt Publishing, 2013), 74–75.

288. Character Lab Card, https://cdn.characterlab.org/assets/Character-Growth-Card-8a9b995138cfd2572a42c2d34ba958e340211cde8ba2a1e80ab44887fb69c671.pdf.

289. Duckworth, *Grit*, 269.

290. Ibid., 139.

291. Ibid., 245.

292. Carol Dweck, *Mindset: The New Psychology of Success* (New York: Ballantine Books, 2008), 7.

293. Ibid., 46.

294. Character Lab Card, https://cdn.characterlab.org/assets/Character-Growth-Card-8a9b995138cfd2572a42c2d34ba958e340211cde8ba2a1e80ab44887fb69c671.pdf.

295. Deborah Meier, "Explaining KIPP's 'SLANT,'" *Education Week*, April 11, 2013, http://blogs.edweek.org/edweek/Bridging-Differences/2013/04/slant_and_the_golden_rule.html.

296. Resources page at *Bit of Grit*, http://www.bitofgrit.com/resources

297. Stephen Fishman and Louise McCarthy, *John Dewey and the Philosophy and Practice of Hope* (Urbana: University of Illinois Press, 2007), 95.

298. Valerie Maholmes, *Fostering Resilience and Well-Being in Children and Families: Why Hope Still Matters* (New York: Oxford University Press, 2014), 14.

299. Ibid., 14.

300. Mike Rose, *Why School? Reclaiming Education for All of Us* (New York: New Press, 2014); Tough, *How Children Succeed*, xv; Mikhail Zinshteyn, July, 23, 2015, "What Does it Mean to have 'Grit' in the Classroom?," *The Atlantic*, http://www.theatlantic.com/education/archive/2015/07/what-grit-looks-like-in-the-classroom/399197/.

301. Martin Seligman, *Learned Optimism: How to Change Your Mind and Your Life* (New York: Vintage, 2006).

302. Tough, *How Children Succeed*, 48.

303. Seligman, *Learned Optimism*, 48; Duckworth, *Grit*, 192.

304. McKibben, Sarah. "Seeing Beyond the Glass Half Full," *Education Update*, 57, no. (2015): 3–5, with this quote on pages 4–5.

305. Groopman, *The Anatomy of Hope*, 199.

306. Ibid., 203.

307. Paul Stoltz, *Grit: The New Science of What It Takes to Persevere* (Climb Strong Press, 2014), 2.

308. Ibid., 45.

309. Ibid., 11.

310. Paul G. Stoltz, *Adversity Quotient: Turning Obstacles into Opportunities* (Hoboken, NJ: John Wiley & Sons, 1997).

311. Angela Duckworth and Lauren Eskreis-Winkler, April 2013, "True Grit," *Observer*, https://www.psychologicalscience.org/ index.php/publications/observer/2013/april-13/true-grit.html; Vicki Davis, January 9, 2014, "True Grit: The

Best Measure of Success and How to Teach it," http://www.edutopia.org/blog/true-grit-measure-teach-success-vicki-davis

312. Tovia Smith, "Does Teaching Kids to Get 'Gritty' Help Them Get Ahead?" *National Public Radio*, March 17, 2014, http://www.npr.org/sections/ed/2014/03/17/290089998/does-teaching-kids-to-get-gritty-help-them-get-ahead; Tovia Smith, March 17, 2014, "On the Syllabus: Lessons in Grit," *National Public Radio*, http://www.npr.org/2014/03/17/290894364/on-the-syllabus-lessons-in-grit.

313. Linda Kaplan Thaler and Robin Koval, *Grit to Great* (New York: Crown Publishing, 2015).

314. Daniel Engber, "Is 'Grit' Really the Key to Success?" *Slate*, May 8, 2016.

315. Duckworth, *Grit*, 237.

316. Kalli Rimfield, Yulia Kovas, Philip S. Dale, and Robert Plomin, "True Grit and Genetics: Predicting Academic Achievement from Personality," *Journal of Personality and Social Psychology*, 111(5), 780–789 (February 11, 2016).

317. Sarah D. Sparks, "'Grit' May Not Spur Creative Success, Scholars Say," *Education Week*, August 19, 2014, http://www.edweek.org/ew/articles/2014/08/20/01grit.h34.html.

318. Rimfield et al., "True Grit and Genetics."

319. Angela Duckworth, Teri A. Kirby, Anton Gollwitzer, Gabriele Oettingen, "From Fantasy to Action: Mental Contrasting with Implementations (MCII) Improves Academic Performance in Children," *School Psychological and Personality Science*, 4, no. 6 (2013): 745–753, http://spp.sagepub.com/content/4/6/745.

320. Anya Kamenetz, "MacArthur 'Genius' Angela Duckworth Responds to a New Critique of Grit," *National Public Radio*, May 25, 2016, http://www.npr.org/sections/ed/2016/05/25/479172868/angela-duckworth-responds-to-a-new-critique-of-grit.

321. My appreciation to Lori Foote for pointing out these differing aspects of socioeconomic status.

322. For more on the possible racist elements of grit, see Benjamin Herold, "Is 'Grit' Racist?" *Education Week*, January 24, 2015, and Perry Andre, "Black and Brown Boys Don't Need to Learn Grit: They Need Schools to Stop Being Racist," *The Root*, May 2, 2016.

323. Ariana Gonzalez Stokas, "A Genealogy of Grit: Education in the New Gilded Age," *Educational Theory*, 65, no. 5 (2015): 513–528, 520.

324. Stitzlein, *Teaching for Dissent*.

325. Gonzalez Stokas, "A Genealogy of Grit."

326. Linda Kaplan Thaler and Robin Koval, *Grit to Great: How Perseverance, Passion, and Pluck Take You from Ordinary to Extraordinary* (New York: Crown Business, 2015).

327. Fishman and McCarthy, *John Dewey*, 43.

328. Garrison, Jim, "A Review of John Dewey and the Philosophy and Practice of Hope," *Teachers College Record*, February 22, 2008.

329. Duckworth, *Grit*.

330. Ibid., 174; Seligman, *Learned Optimism*, 4–5.

331. Maholmes, *Fostering Resilience and Well-Being in Children and Families*.

332. Rick Snyder, *The Pscyhology of Hope* (New York: Free Press, 1994).

333. Dewey, "Democracy and Education," 26.

334. John Dewey, *The Later Works, 1925–1953, Vol. 14*, edited by J. A. Boydston (Carbondale: Southern Illinois University Press, 1981), 226.

335. For more, see Gert Biesta, "Education and the Democratic Person: Towards a Political Conception of Democratic Education," *Teachers College Record*, 109, no. 3 (2007): 740–769.

336. I am borrowing parts of this paragraph from my discussion of citizenship education within my book Sarah M. Stitzlein, *American Public Education and the Responsibility of Its Citizens: Supporting Democracy in an Age of Accountability* (New York: Oxford Unversity Press), 2017.

337. I recognize that some grit proponents do not situate teaching grit within citizenship education, but I contend that its goals of personal and character development fit within that larger umbrella and that social studies classrooms are a more appropriate home for grit education than other traditional subject areas.

Chapter 6

338. I'm aware of some of the ethical critiques of this activity and do not mean to suggest that I'm backing that particular approach. Rather, I note it as a very well-known example, likely recognized by my lay readers, that demonstrates making a larger social issue a lived and meaningful experience right in the classroom, including for white children who might not otherwise have known the felt experience of racial and other forms of discrimination. To its credit, the simulation may also enable empathy and the sort of imagination across racial boundaries that I call for elsewhere in this chapter.

339. Laura Parker, "'Biggest Case of the Planet' Pits Kids vs. Climate Change," *National Geographic*, November 9, 2018, https://news.nationalgeographic.com/2017/03/kids-sue-us-government-climate-change/.

340. Adrian Horton, Dream McClinton, and Lauren Aratani, "Adults Failed to Take Climate Action: Meet Young Activists Stepping Up," *The Guardian*, March 4, 2019. Abroad, we see sizable youth protests in Europe and Australia, "Climate Change Protests Staged by Children," *BBC News*, February 15, 2019, https://www.bbc.com/news/av/47254809/climate-change-protests-staged-by-children. Examples of student inquiry and change range from student-led climate and recycling clubs in schools to NASA Climate Kids, https://climate.kids.nasa.gov/how-to-help and National Geographic's Climate Reality Project, among others. Some California students organized a conference to look at various ways to solve climate change and engage in action about it, "Teens Organize Conference to Address Climate Change," *AP News*, October 26, 2018, https://www.apnews.com/ec50b5cbd5412e34e5c058b67a50b5dd; while other students are turning to technology and innovation to propose solutions, "Young Innovators for Climate Change—How the Youth Is Tackling Climate Change, One Innovation at a Time," http://climatetracker.org/young-innovators-climate-change-youth-tackling-climate-change-one-innovation-time/.

341. Guest speakers, in particular, while providing a more human and perhaps moving take on an issue, also present potential harm when it comes to this issue, which is deeply tied to a history of racism and slavery. Speakers would need to be carefully chosen and facilitated by the teacher, with careful attention to comments perceived as hurtful by students.

342. Benjamin Wallace-Wells, "The Fight over Virginia's Confederate Monuments," *New Yorker*, May 31, 2018, accessed September 12, 2018, https://www.newyorker.com/magazine/2017/12/04/the-fight-over-virginias-confederate-monuments.

343. Coates, mentioned earlier, is one of those who has already spoken out about such harms. Ta-Nehisi Coates, "Take Down the Confederate Flag-Now," *The Atlantic*, January 5, 2016, accessed September 12, 2018, https://www.theatlantic.com/politics/archive/2015/06/take-down-the-confederate-flag-now/396290/.

344. Yoni Appelbaum, "Why Is the Confederate Flag Still There?" *The Atlantic*, June 22, 2015, accessed September 12, 2018, https://www.theatlantic.com/politics/archive/2015/06/why-is-the-flag-still-there/396431/.

345. Levinson, *Leave No Citizen Behind*, chapter 6.

346. Victoria McGeer, "Trust, Hope, and Empowerment," *Australian Journal of Philosophy*, 86 (2008): 237–254, 248–249.

347. Peter Levine and Kei Kawashima-Ginsberg, "The Republic is (Still) at Risk—And Civics Is Part of the Solution," *Medford: Tufts University, September*, 21 (2017): 5.

348. Felicia M. Sullivan and Surbi Godsay, "A National Survey of Civics and U.S. Government Teachers," *CIRCLE Fact Sheet*, The Center for Information and Research on Civic Learning and Engagement, Tufts University, June 2014, 4, http://www.academia.edu/10203684/A_National_Survey_of_Civics_and_U.S._Government_Teachers.

349. Thanks to Lisa Sibbett for bringing this study to my attention. David Backer, "The Distortion of Discussion," *Issues in Teacher Education*, 27, no. 1 (2018): 3–16.

350. Dewey, "Democracy and Education," 97–98.

351. Ibid., 101.

352. Ibid., 188–189.

353. Ibid., 6.

354. John Dewey, "Experience and Nature," in *The Middle Works, 1899–1924*, vol. 9, edited by J. A. Boydston (Carbondale: Southern Illinois University Press, 1980 [1925]), 141.

355. John Dewey, "Democracy and Education," 12.

356. Green, *Pragmatism and Social Hope*, 235.

357. Dewey, *Creative Democracy*, 228.

358. Barak Rosenshine, "Principles of Instruction: Research-Based Strategies That All Teachers Should Know," *American Educator*, 78, no. 3 (2012): 30.

359. Ginwright, *Hope and Healing in Urban Education*, 24.

360. Shade, *Habits of Hope*.

361. Ibid.

362. Bovens, "The Value of Hope," 676.

363. Amy Gutmann, *Democratic Education* (Princeton, NJ: Princeton University Press, 1999).

364. Dewey, "Democracy and Education," 105.

365. Thanks to Lori Foote for pointing out the relevance of those particular curricular standards to me.

366. Founders of March for our Lives, *Glimmer of Hope: How Tragedy Sparked a Movement* (New York: Penguin Random House, 2018), see especially page 77.

367. Rebecca Solnit, "Protest and Persist: Why Giving Up Hope Is Not an Option," *The Guardian*, March 13, 2017, accessed September 12, 2018, https://www.theguardian.com/world/2017/mar/13/protest-persist-hope-trump-activism-anti-nuclear-movement.

368. Joshua Foa Dienstag, *Pessimism: Philosophy, Ethic, Spirit* (Princeton, NJ: Princeton University Press, 2006), 17.

369. Dewey, *Human Nature and Conduct*, 132.

370. Christopher LeBron, "Thoughts on Racial Democratic Education and Moral Virtue," *Theory and Research in Education*, 13, no. 2 (2015): 155–164, 160–161.

371. WVS Database, accessed September 12, 2018, http://www.worldvaluessurvey.org/WVSContents.jsp.

372. http://www.storytellersproject.com/national/.

373. I borrow this example from colleague and long-time elementary teacher, Lori Foote, who also helped me develop many of the ideas related to teaching hope in this chapter.

374. Green, *Pragmatism and Social Hope*.

375. *Hope Photographs*, edited by Alice Rose George and Lee Marks (New York: Thames and Hudson, 1998).

376. I am most indebted to Sigal Ben-Porath for her excellent work on shared fate. Sigal Ben-Porath, "Education for Shared Fate Citizenship," in *Education, Justice, and Democracy*, edited by Danielle Allen and Rob Reich (Chicago: University of Chicago Press, 2013), 80–100.

377. Mary Annette Pember, "Cowboys and Indians Unite against Keystone XL," *CNN*, April 27, 2014, accessed November 28, 2018, https://www.cnn.com/2014/04/27/opinion/pember-keystone-cowboys-indians/index.html.

378. Shane J. Lopez, *Making Hope Happen* (New York: Atria Books, 2013), 139.

379. Amy Shuffleton, "The Politics of Working Together," *Educational Theory* 68, no. 2 (2018): 147–160.

380. Levine and Kawashima-Ginsberg, "The Republic Is (Still) at Risk."

381. Glaude, *Democracy in Black*, 204.

382. Sullivan and Godsay, "A National Survey."

383. "Civic Learning through Action: The Case of Generation Citizen," *CIRCLE Report*, The Center for Information and Research on Civic Learning and Engagement, Tufts University, June 2013, http://www.civicyouth.org/wp-content/uploads/2013/07/Generation-Citizen-Fact-Sheet-July-1-Final.pdf.

384. I am grateful to Lisa Sibbett for helping me think through these dimensions of trust and mistrust.

385. For more along these lines of trust, see McGeer, "Trust, Hope, and Empowerment."

386. Brett Johnson, "Overcoming 'Gloom and Doom': Empowering Students on Courses in Social Justice, Injustice, and Inequality," *Teaching Sociology*, 33 (2005): 44–58, 46.

387. For more, see Mark Warren drawing on the work of Jane Mansbridge. Mark Warren, *Democracy and Trust* (Cambridge, Cambridge University Press, 2010), 17.

388. Allison Penelope Anoll, "Creating Citizens: Civics Education, Civic Socialization and Engagement Patterns," dissertation, College of William and Mary (2009), 44.

389. Sean Ginwright describes these outlets in his book *Hope and Healing in Urban Education*, 20.

390. Johari R. Shuck and Robert J. Helfenbein, "Civic Identity, Public Education, and the African-American Community in Indianapolis: Mending the Fracture," *Journal of Civic Literacy*, 2 no. 1 (2015): 24–42.

391. Jean L. Cohen and Andrew Arato, *Civil Society and Political Theory* (Cambridge, MA: MIT Press, 1992).

392. I'm following Knight Abowitz in her initial description of civil society here. Kathleen Knight Abowitz, *Publics for Public Schools: Legitimacy, Democracy, and Leadership* (Boulder, CO: Paradigm Publishers, 2014).

393. Robert J. Lacey, *American Pragmatism and Democratic Faith* (Dekalb: Northern Illinois University Press, 2008), 207.

394. I take much of my discussion of civil society here from chapter 7 in my book *American Public Education and the Responsibility of Its Citizens: Supporting Democracy in an Age of Accountability* (New York: Oxford University Press, 2017).

395. Rachel Gabel, "Kansas Woman's Letter to AOC Brings MSNBC to Her Ranch," *The Fence Post*, February 25, 2019.

396. "Statement from Nebraska Farm Bureau President Steve Nelson Regarding Congress 'Green New Deal,'" Nebraska Farm Bureau Newsroom, February 8, 2019.

397. Skocpol, *Diminished Democracy*, 176.

398. For more along these lines, see Judith Green, *Pragmatism and Social Hope*, 98.

399. I borrow this question from Peter Levin, a professor at Tufts University.

400. Some of these obstacles are documented in Jonathan Zimmerman and Emily Robertson, *The Case for Contention: Teaching Controversial Issues in American Schools* (Chicago, IL: University of Chicago Press).

Index